HERO TALES

VOLUME III

Books by Dave and Neta Jackson

~~~~~~~~~~~~~~~~~~~~~~~~~~~

Hero Tales: A Family Treasury of True Stories
From the Lives of Christian Heroes (Volumes I, II, and III)

Trailblazer Books

Gladys Aylward • *Flight of the Fugitives*
Mary McLeod Bethune • *Defeat of the Ghost Riders*
William & Catherine Booth • *Kidnapped by River Rats*
Governor William Bradford • *The Mayflower Secret*
John Bunyan • *Traitor in the Tower*
Amy Carmichael • *The Hidden Jewel*
Peter Cartwright • *Abandoned on the Wild Frontier*
Elizabeth Fry • *The Thieves of Tyburn Square*
Sheldon Jackson • *The Gold Miners' Rescue*
Adoniram & Ann Judson • *Imprisoned in the Golden City*
David Livingstone • *Escape from the Slave Traders*
Martin Luther • *Spy for the Night Riders*
Dwight L. Moody • *Danger on the Flying Trapeze*
Samuel Morris • *Quest for the Lost Prince*
George Müller • *The Bandit of Ashley Downs*
John Newton • *The Runaway's Revenge*
Florence Nightingale • *The Drummer Boy's Battle*
Nate Saint • *The Fate of the Yellow Woodbee*
Menno Simons • *The Betrayer's Fortune*
Mary Slessor • *Trial by Poison*
Hudson Taylor • *Shanghaied to China*
Harriet Tubman • *Listen for the Whippoorwill*
William Tyndale • *The Queen's Smuggler*
John Wesley • *The Chimney Sweep's Ransom*
Marcus & Narcissa Whitman • *Attack in the Rye Grass*
David Zeisberger • *The Warrior's Challenge*

HERO
TALES

VOLUME III

DAVE & NETA
JACKSON

BETHANY HOUSE PUBLISHERS
MINNEAPOLIS, MINNESOTA 55438

Hero Tales, Volume III: A Family Treasury of True Stories From the Lives of Christian Heroes
Copyright © 1998
Dave and Neta Jackson

Cover design by Peter Glöege. Interior illustrations by Toni Auble.

Published by Bethany House Publishers
A Ministry of Bethany Fellowship International
11370 Hampshire Avenue South
Minneapolis, Minnesota 55438
www.bethanyhouse.com

Printed in the United States of America

ISBN 1–55661–712–7 (Volume I)
ISBN 1–55661–713–5 (Volume II)
ISBN 1–55661–018–1 (Volume III)

Library of Congress Cataloging-in-Publication Data

Jackson, Dave.
    Hero tales: a family treasury of true stories from the lives of Christian heroes / Dave and Neta Jackson.
        p. cm.
    Summary: Presents biographies of fifteen missionaries, evangelists, and other Christian heroes who worked courageously to share the Gospel with others.

    1. Christian biography—Juvenile literature. 2. Missionaries—Biography—Juvenile literature. [1. Christian biography. 2. Missionaries.] I. Jackson, Neta. II. Title.
BR1704.J33   1996
270'.092'2—dc20
[B]   96–25230
                                                                              CIP
                                                                               AC

For Trisha Washington—
who has faced life heroically
from the day she was born.

CONTENTS ❧

CONTENTS

MARY McLEOD BETHUNE

———— ❧ ————

Teacher of Head,
Hands, and Heart

Sam and Patsy McLeod and ten of their children were born into slavery on a cotton plantation in Mayesville, South Carolina. But the Emancipation Proclamation of 1863 ended five generations of slavery for the McLeod family, and their fifteenth child, Mary Jane, who came into the world on July 10, 1875, was born free.

But "born free" for blacks in the South didn't necessarily mean "equal." As Mary struggled to understand her world, she decided the main difference between white people and black people was that white people could read. To go to school became her burning passion. When a school for black children was finally started in Mayesville, eleven-year-old Mary became an eager student.

Within a few years, the teacher recommended her for a scholarship to Scotia Seminary in Concord, North Carolina—a school for the daughters of "freedmen"—where Mary studied literature, Greek, Latin, the Bible, and American democracy. She soaked up knowledge like a thirsty sponge, but she also wanted to give back what she learned. Deciding to become a missionary to her own people back in

Africa, she attended Moody Bible Institute in Chicago. But when she graduated and applied to the Presbyterian Mission Board, she was told, "We have no openings for a colored missionary in Africa."

It was the bitterest disappointment of Mary's life. But it was also a turning point. If she couldn't go to Africa, she would teach her people right here at home in the South.

While teaching at Kendell Institute in Sumter, Georgia, she met a handsome young teacher named Albertus Bethune, whom she married in 1898. A year later Albertus Jr. was born.

But Mary's dream of "giving back" deepened. She was glad for the black colleges that were being formed at the turn of the century—but what good was a college when so many black children in the South couldn't even read? In her mind was a school where young girls and boys would not only learn useful trades, but the arts and sciences and the rights and responsibilities of citizenship. "Greek and a toothbrush!" she'd laugh when someone asked about her beliefs on education.

Wealthy whites were going south to Florida during the harsh northern winters. This meant jobs for blacks working on the new railroad and putting up the new hotels. Shantytowns grew up for these workers near resort towns like Daytona Beach. This became Mary McLeod Bethune's mission field. She determined to build a school to teach the head (classical education), hands (practical education), and heart (spiritual education). In 1904 she started with five little girls . . . and by 1923, her vision had become Bethune-Cookman College in Daytona, Florida.

When Mrs. Bethune died in 1955, she had not only served as an inspiration to thousands of young black people but also as an advisor to President Franklin D. Roosevelt. She worked tirelessly for the Urban League, the NAACP, the National Council of Negro Women, the National Youth Administration, and the Federal Council of Negro Affairs. In her will she stated: "I leave you love . . . I leave you hope . . . I leave you a thirst for education . . . I leave, finally, a responsibility to our young people."

FAITH
"But...Where's the School?"

Thirteen-year-old Mary McLeod stood wide-eyed and open-mouthed, bag in hand, at the gate of Scotia Seminary for the Daughters of Freedmen (former slaves) in Concord, North Carolina. She had never imagined such a wonderful place. Brick buildings with white pillars stood among tree-shaded lawns. Surely someone would pinch her and tell her it was all a mistake. She didn't belong here.

Then she remembered. A Quaker woman out in Colorado had offered a scholarship to a Negro girl who would "make good," and Mary's teacher, Miss Wilson, had recommended Mary. She had been praying day and night for the chance to get an education. And now here she was. "Victory through faith!"

Mary threw herself into her studies: Greek, Latin, literature, Bible, and American democracy. When she finished the high school course, she took Scotia's Normal course to become a teacher herself. She wanted to give back everything she'd learned—and someday she'd have a school of her own, a school like Scotia. Except she would take her school to where the children were, the children who lived in the little shantytowns and back roads of the South, who didn't know how to read.

After graduation from Scotia, Mary accepted several teaching assignments in the South. But she was frustrated at the limited education black children were being offered. In her mind, her dream school began to grow.

1. She'd fill it with song to express the longings of her people.
2. It would look like Scotia, with beautiful buildings and grounds.
3. It would train boys and girls to work for a living, learning all sorts of skills and trades.
4. It would give all the world's learning, including the arts and sciences.
5. It would teach the duties and privileges of citizenship.
6. It would be a living part of the community—reaching out in service, building up her people to take their rightful place as productive citizens.

While teaching in Palatka, Florida, with her husband, Albertus, and little boy, Albert Jr., Mary noticed that many black families were following the new railroad down the leg of Florida, hoping for jobs. Shantytowns of railroad workers and hotel workers were growing up alongside wealthy winter resorts such as Daytona Beach. But who was going to teach their children?

With only $1.50 to her name, Mary and her little family set out for Daytona. Now she had a goal. Now she had a destination. This was where she would begin her school. "Victory through faith!" she told herself.

Starting with just five little girls and a four-room house that she rented for eleven dollars a month, Mrs. Bethune named her school "The Daytona Educational and Industrial Institute for Girls." As more and more girls came, the little house quickly became too small. She needed land. She needed to build. But where would she get the money?

Nothing, Mary Bethune reminded herself, was ever accomplished without acting in faith. Forming the girls into a choir, she began taking them to churches and hotels as a way to advertise the school and raise money. At one hotel, she met a distinguished gentleman with white hair who seemed genuinely interested in her description of the school. Happily, Mrs. Bethune invited him to come for a visit.

A few days later, a sleek black car drove up in front of the shabby little house. The white-haired gentleman got out and looked around. With curious girls crowding at the windows, Mrs. Bethune went out to meet him.

"But . . . where's the school?" he said, bewildered.

Mrs. Bethune smiled broadly. "In my mind and in my heart, Mr. Gamble! What you see is just the seed, which will soon grow. But we need a board of trustees, with men like you who also have a vision for what the school can become. Mr. Gamble, will you become our first trustee?"

Now Mr. Gamble was smiling, too. "I like your attitude, Mrs. Bethune," he said. "I would be honored to be the first trustee of your school."

Mr. Gamble—of Proctor and Gamble—became a valuable friend of Mary McLeod Bethune's school, and the first building to be built was named "Faith Hall."

Faith is claiming victory and acting on what you believe God wants you to do.

FROM GOD'S WORD:

Everyone who is a child of God conquers the world. And this is the victory that conquers the world—our faith (1 John 5:4).

LET'S TALK ABOUT IT:

1. What was Mrs. Bethune's way of "giving back" what she'd been given?
2. Why do you think Mrs. Bethune's motto became "Victory through faith"?
3. What is the difference between "having faith" and "acting in faith"?

DILIGENCE
No Such Thing as
a Menial Task

~~~~~~~~~~~~~~~~~~~~~~~~~~~~

Welcome, girls!" Mary McLeod Bethune faced her first class of girls, her broad, dark face beaming. "Enter these doors to learn. Depart to serve."

The little school in a rented house on the edge of a shantytown in Daytona, Florida, didn't look like much. They had no school supplies and few books. Mrs. Bethune had no money, and some of the girls couldn't pay the fifty cents per week tuition. But the lack of money and supplies didn't stop Mrs. Bethune. Organizing the girls into scavenger teams, they combed the alleys and town dump for useable items like cooking pots and pounded the dents out of them. A packing box served as a desk. Charcoal splinters were used as pencils. Spanish moss hanging from the big oak trees was stuffed into cotton ticks for mattresses. Old clothes were made over to fit the girls.

Mornings were given to book studies: literature, Bible, Latin, history. Afternoons found the girls doing housekeeping chores and learning practical skills, such as how to bake pies, set a proper table, tend a garden, and sew up curtains for the windows. "We seek to educate the head, the hands, and the heart," Mrs. Bethune gently reminded the girls when they complained about having to scrub the floors again.

But not everyone was happy with Mrs. Bethune's philosophy of education. Some of her critics were black people like herself. "You're teaching the girls to do menial (lowly) work!" they fussed. "We don't want to be servants and laborers anymore! Our children need philosophy and science and the arts!"

"They need both," she countered. "Yes, our people need to reach for their fullest potential, but in the meantime, they need to make a living and take advantage of whatever opportunities are open to them. Besides," she huffed, "there is no such thing as menial work—only a menial attitude."

The Daytona Educational and Industrial Institute grew from five girls to twenty to two hundred . . . and more. Even though Mrs. Bethune went knocking on the doors of blacks and whites alike seeking support for the school, she and the girls worked hard to support themselves. They planted a vegetable garden and grew beans, carrots, sugarcane, strawberries, and sweet potatoes. Besides food for their own table, they sold fresh vegetables to the local tourists. The girls made sweet potato pies and sold them to the hungry railroad workers eager for some home cooking. Some of the older girls hired themselves out as helpers in wealthy white homes as a way to support themselves while getting an education.

"Oh, Mrs. Bethune," they wailed one day. "How will we ever get these clean?" They showed her a pile of fine white linen tablecloths.

"Boil them," she instructed.

The girls looked at one another. Boil them? That meant making a fire out in the yard and waiting while the big tub of water heated up. So much work!

Later in the day, Mrs. Bethune stopped by and noticed dripping wet tablecloths pinned to the clothesline. The girls were taking off their aprons and looking relieved that the task was finally done.

But Mrs. Bethune came right to the point. "Did you boil them?"

Guiltily the girls hung their heads.

Down came the tablecloths from the line. A fire was made, the water boiled, and the cloths went into the pot. "You can never take a shortcut to thoroughness," she told the girls firmly. It was a lesson all the students in Mrs. Bethune's school learned, whether they were conjugating Latin verbs or doing laundry.

Diligence is putting forth your best effort,
regardless of the task.

FROM GOD'S WORD:

Whatever work you do, do your best (Ecclesiastes 9:10a).

LET'S TALK ABOUT IT:

1. What do you think Mrs. Bethune meant when she said, "There is no such thing as menial work—only a menial attitude"?

2. What was the result of Mrs. Bethune's educating not only the "head," but also the "hands" and the "hearts" of her students?

3. What kind of work tempts you to take shortcuts? Homework? Chores? Why?

DIGNITY
"'Whosoever' Means You!"

rs. Mary McLeod Bethune opened her Bible. Sitting in front of her in orderly rows were girls with freshly scrubbed ebony skin, their soft, dark hair brushed and braided, their dark blue skirts and white blouses—the school's uniform— clean and neat. Some of them were the daughters of clergymen and shopkeepers; others were daughters of railroad workers and day laborers. It didn't matter to Mrs. Bethune. All these girls needed an education. Even more, they needed to know their worth before God after years— centuries—of living in a society that told them they were an inferior race.

"'For God so loved the world,'" Mrs. Bethune read in her rich contralto voice,"' that he gave his only begotten Son, that whosoever believeth in him should not perish, but have everlasting life.'" She looked up at the eager faces in front of her. "Did you hear that word, 'whosoever'? That whosoever means you! God loves you so much He sent His Son, Jesus, to die for you. Not just white people. Not just rich people. You! This is where your human dignity comes from—from God, our Creator and Savior."

Mary McLeod Bethune was a good example of dignity. That means she treated everyone, black and white alike, as she would like to be treated. One day she was out knocking on doors in the neighborhood, asking for help for the school. An old white woman came to the door wearing a dirty apron. "Yes, I've heard about your school," she said. "Right nice idea—though I don't 'spect you'll teach 'em much beyond third grade. That's all my pastor says the colored can learn."

Mrs. Bethune winced but did not react to the insult. "I notice you have a cow," she said. "Do you have some milk to spare for the girls?"

"Why, matter of fact, I do," said the old woman. "I churn butter to make ends meet . . . end up having to throw a lot of buttermilk away. You just send up your girls with a pail, and I'll give you all the buttermilk you can use."

Mrs. Bethune smiled broadly. "Thank you very much!"

"Say," said the woman, "I s'pose you can read, being a teacher 'n all. I've . . . uh . . . mislaid my glasses, and I wonder if you could read this letter my son sent me."

Mrs. Bethune—a college graduate—guessed that the woman probably couldn't read herself, but graciously she said nothing and read the woman's letter. It wasn't in her nature to return insult for insult.

Another day, as she was once again knocking on doors telling about the needs of the school, the family happened to be having lunch. Thinking she was a common beggar, the woman said, "Why don't you go into the kitchen, and Ida will give you some lunch."

"Thank you, no," said Mrs. Bethune and moved on to the next house.

The old couple next door was also at lunch, but they invited her to sit down and eat with them. Mrs. Bethune gladly accepted the invitation. While they were enjoying coffee, the woman next door dropped in. Seeing Mrs. Bethune sitting at the table with her hosts, her face reddened. But all Mrs. Bethune did was smile at her graciously.

When young Mary was growing up, white people always called black people by their first names, like children. She never forgot the first time she heard a black person—her first teacher—introduce herself as "Miss Wilson." It gave her a thrill of pride that she resolved to not only extend to others, but to require for herself. After marriage, she always introduced herself as Mrs. Bethune. Many years later, in 1934, she was a delegate to the Southern Conference for Human Welfare. After she proposed an amendment, the chairwoman announced, "Mary's amendment is accepted."

Mrs. Bethune rose and said with simple dignity, "My name is Mrs. Mary McLeod Bethune, and the secretary should record it so."

Dignity means recognizing the basic worth God gives each one of us, and treating one another with respect.

FROM GOD'S WORD:
So God created human beings in his image. In the image of God he created them (Genesis 1:27a). Show respect for all people (1 Peter 2:17a).

LET'S TALK ABOUT IT:
1. Why was it important for Mrs. Bethune to teach her students that they had dignity as human beings?
2. In what way did Mrs. Bethune show that dignity was a two-way street?
3. Discuss ways you can act with dignity yourself as well as treat others with dignity.

WILLIAM BRADFORD

Puritan of Plymouth

William Bradford, born in 1590, was the only son of a yeoman (pronounced "yo-man") family (middle-class farmers) in Austerfield,
England, but his parents died while he was still quite young. A sickly
boy, he learned to read and loved learning. At age sixteen, he heard a
controversial preacher teach the "Puritan Principles" of personal holi-
ness and separation of church and state. Disobeying his uncles, who told
him not to associate with these "Separatists," William began attending a
Puritan congregation at Scrooby, where he met Elder William Brewster,
who became the father and mentor William had never had.

King James I made life difficult for these "reformers." When
Brewster and others were arrested and fined for being "disobedient in
religion," the Scrooby congregation moved to Leyden, Holland, which
promised political and religious freedom. In Leyden, Bradford took
advantage of the university library to complete his self-education. At
twenty-three, already a respected member of the congregation, he married sixteen-year-old Dorothy May. Two years later they had a son, John.

But the Puritans were first and foremost Englishmen, and they read-
ily left Holland when the opportunity came to establish an English

colony in the New World. Supported by the Merchant Adventurers—a group of profit-hungry businessmen—the Puritans sailed for their "Promised Land" in September 1620 on an overcrowded ship called the *Mayflower*.

Within sight of land, the colonists drew up an agreement to govern themselves, known as the Mayflower Compact. The seeds for democracy were planted before they ever set foot on dry ground.

While Bradford and the other men were exploring the shore for a place to build their colony, Dorothy Bradford apparently drowned. More than half the colonists died that first winter of "the terrible sickness." The following spring, Bradford was elected governor of New Plymouth and continued to be reelected for a span of thirty years. Three years after his wife's death, Bradford married Alice Carpenter Southworth, taking in a group of homeless boys, as well as his own children.

William Bradford had a reputation for dealing fairly with both colonists and Indians and lived in peace with their closest neighbors, Chief Massasoit and the Wampanoag tribe, for fifty years. Twice while Bradford was governor, however, Plymouth attacked Indians they perceived as a threat, events that troubled the Separatists who had hopes of "Christianizing" the Indians. Sadly, the history of New England reveals that colonists killed many more Indians than they converted.

In 1630, Bradford began writing his important history, *Of Plymouth Plantation* (originally spelled "Plimoth"). Long after his death in 1657, he represented the vision of the Puritans who came to this country seeking freedom of religion. But his hope for an ongoing community united in the worship of God was never fully realized. Still, the seeds of democracy were planted by these earnest Pilgrims, who laid the groundwork for free people—making their own laws by everyone agreeing on them.

PEACEMAKER
Saving Squanto's Skin

illiam Bradford faced the tall, bare-chested Indian who stood proudly before him. "Hobomok," said Bradford in a questioning tone, "did you know Squanto's nephew came running into the stockade a few hours ago saying the Narragansetts are marching against us? He also thought Chief Massasoit had joined them."

"It cannot be true!" Hobomok answered. "Massasoit is a man of his word. He would not break his treaty with the English." Hobomok's eyes flashed anger. "You say Squanto's nephew brought this news?" The warrior spit in disgust. "Squanto is behind this, telling lies, trying to stir up trouble."

Bradford sighed. He had just been reelected governor of Plymouth Colony for the second year, and now the colony was facing another crisis. He knew Squanto—their friend and interpreter—was jealous of Hobomok, Chief Massasoit's top warrior, who had been sent to live among the English as the chief's ambassador. But he could hardly believe Squanto would stoop this low.

"Then I ask you a favor, Hobomok," said the governor. "Ask your wife to visit the Wampanoag village—pretending she's there for a social visit— and see if Chief Massasoit is preparing for war. Bring us word so that we might know the truth."

Hobomok agreed. Within days his wife returned with the word: Nothing unusual was going on in Chief Massasoit's village.

"That no-good, two-timing scoundrel!" Captain Miles Standish exploded to Bradford when he heard of Squanto's betrayal. The short, stocky captain had never trusted Squanto. "You should kick him out of the colony for—" The captain's attention was suddenly drawn away by several painted warriors who marched into the stockade. "Uh-oh," he said. "Looks like trouble."

The warriors strode up to Bradford and Standish. Their spokesman threw a stack of beaver skins on the ground—a good-faith present—and came right to the point. "Chief Massasoit says Squanto has broken the treaty by trying to stir up trouble between the Wampanoags and English. He demands that you turn Squanto over to him for punishment, just as the treaty says."

Governor Bradford frowned. The treaty with Chief Massasoit was important to their continued peaceful relations. But Squanto's friendship and help had literally saved them from starvation the previous spring. Even if he did deserve punishment, Bradford couldn't just turn him over to be killed. What kind of gratefulness was that?

"It is not the way of the English to sell men's lives for a price," he stalled, refusing the gift of beaver skins. "I will send for Squanto and see what he has to say in his own defense." *And if you're smart, Squanto, you'll take the hint and drop out of sight for a while*, Bradford thought.

But Squanto showed up, protesting his innocence and blaming Hobomok for trying to get him in trouble. As the heated discussion continued, suddenly the cry went up, "A sail! A ship has turned into the bay!"

Seeing this as an opportunity, Bradford said, "I can't possibly decide Squanto's guilt or innocence until we find out whether the ship is friend or foe. This matter will have to wait." With that, he and the other colonists hurried Squanto off and prepared to greet the strange ship. By the time the colonists had discovered that it was a friendly ship and greeted the newcomers, Massasoit's warriors had grown impatient with the delay and left, their mission stalled.

Squanto was safe . . . for now.

⁂

A peacemaker will look for ways to live peaceably with people on both sides of a dispute.

FROM GOD'S WORD:

Try to live in peace with all people (Hebrews 12:14).

LET'S TALK ABOUT IT:

1. In what way was William Bradford caught in the middle of this dispute?
2. What would you have done if you had been in Bradford's shoes?
3. Brainstorm ways to live peaceably with different groups or individuals at school or work who don't get along.

INTEGRITY
Share One
Another's Burdens

~~~~~~~~~~~~~~~~~~~~~~~~~~~~~~~~

illiam Bradford stood in the doorway of his sturdy plank house and watched the people of Plymouth pick their way along the muddy street running through the colony. Their clothes were patched and ragged. The last harvest had been poor, and the faces of the children were thin and pale from a winter with only a small food supply.

For the third year in a row, Bradford had been reelected governor of Plymouth Colony. But the welfare of the colony weighed heavily on his shoulders. Their contract with the Merchant Adventurers, who had paid for their journey on the *Mayflower* and purchased their original supplies, required them to send food and furs back to England for seven years and then divide all property with them. In an attempt to begin repaying their debt, the colonists had loaded a ship with fish, beaver pelts, and corn—but French pirates had taken everything before it ever reached England. Until the Merchant Adventurers received some payment, they refused to send any more supplies.

Bradford watched the men and women going about their chores. It was almost time for the third spring planting, but the people were discouraged. For two years all their efforts had gone toward working the colony gardens. After setting aside just enough food for the colony in the common storehouse, all the profits went to repay the Merchant Adventurers. The man who worked from dawn to dusk got no more for his family than the man who came last and left early.

Bradford smacked the doorpost with his fist. Something had to change if the colony was going to survive!

Calling a meeting of the colony leaders, Bradford laid out his plan. "We will give every family one acre for each man, woman, and child to farm for themselves. Unmarried men and women will also be given one acre each, but they will be assigned to a family so they don't have to work alone."

"But aren't we breaking the terms of our contract with the Merchant Adventurers?" someone asked nervously.

"Yes, and I take full responsibility for doing so. Our survival is at stake! I believe people will be more willing to work if each family is filling its own cupboards. But we must still give a part of our harvest, the furs we trap, and the wood we cut to repay our debt."

The colonists eagerly voted to accept the new plan. Bradford was right; working to support their own families gave them new energy to work. All agreed to work part of the time to help repay the colony's debt. At the end of seven years, Bradford bargained with the Merchant Adventurers to buy all rights to the colony for 1,800 English pounds. This meant they still had a debt to pay, but Bradford and the other leaders agreed to pay it themselves in exchange for a larger share of the colony's trade.

Years later, some of the colonists complained that Bradford had more land than his fair share. The Council for New England had actually given some land to him for his long service as governor. However, in a town meeting in March 1639, Bradford offered to divide the land in question among all the freemen of Plymouth. He decided that sharing the land was better for the colony than jealousy and conflict.

Finally, in 1648, Bradford and the other leaders paid off the final debt to the Merchant Adventurers. They were free!

Integrity requires us to take responsibility for any debts
we have agreed to pay.

FROM GOD'S WORD:

Pay all your debts, except the debt of love for others
(Romans 13:8, NLT).

LET'S TALK ABOUT IT:

1. How did Bradford take responsibility for the debt owed to the Merchant Adventurers, even though he decided to break (or change) the contract?
2. In what way did Bradford pay a "debt of love" as Romans 13:8 talks about?
3. Do you owe a debt to anyone that seems unfair or hard to pay? How can you take responsibility to clear the debt?

FAITH
A Slippery Sea of Mud

~~~~~~~~~~~~~~~~~~~~~~~~~~~~~~~~~~

William Bradford bent down and took a handful of dirt. It was dry and crumbly and sifted like sand through his fingers. He squinted into the bright sunshine at the parched fields of corn, beans, squash, peas, and potatoes the colonists had planted so hopefully that spring of 1623. All the plants drooped like sad children being sent to bed without supper.

"What are we going to do, Hobomok?" Bradford said to one of his companions. "It is July already, and we have had no rain for six, maybe seven weeks."

The tall Wampanoag warrior shook his head. "I cannot remember such a dry spell since I was a little grasshopper."

Elder Brewster, his gray hair hanging long and thin under his dusty felt hat, put a hand on Bradford's shoulder. "I think we must humble ourselves and declare a day of fasting and prayer for rain."

The governor thought about this. No one in the colony worked on the Sabbath, but could they afford another day with no labor? It took the efforts of everyone six days a week to gather berries, catch fish, hoe weeds, haul water, wash clothes, build houses, chop firewood, mend shoes—just to stay alive in this wilderness. But life and death were in God's hands, and there was only one Person who could bring the rain.

"You are right, my friend," Bradford said. "We will declare a day of fasting and prayer, asking Almighty God in heaven to have mercy on us." Then he grinned. "Fasting won't be that hard since we have so little food already!"

On the appointed day, all the residents of Plymouth—men, women, boys, girls, babies, English and Indian—trudged up the hill along the dry, rutted street to the fort, which looked out over Cape Cod Bay. The sturdy fort served as a fortress in case of danger, as well as a meeting-house. The men and boys sat on one side of the main room on plain wooden benches. The women and girls sat on the other side.

All day long the colonists and their Indian friends sang hymns, read the Scriptures, and prayed. When the children whimpered from thirst, one of the boys ran with a bucket to Town Brook, which had been shrinking day by day, and hauled back a bucket of water to pass around. The air was hot and still inside the boxlike fort as the sun moved slowly in its arc across the sky.

Finally, as the sun dipped down behind the trees and the sky darkened, Elder Brewster brought the day-long prayer meeting to a close. As the tired people walked out of the fort and started down the hill, William Bradford looked up at the sky. Clouds were gathering and a breeze ruffled his hair.

Sometime during the night a gentle rain began. Bradford got out of bed and stood in the doorway of his thatched-roof house, letting the rain fall on his face. "Thank you, Father in heaven, for your mercy on your people," he prayed aloud, his heart nearly bursting with gratefulness and thanksgiving. This rain meant the difference between life and death.

The gentle rain continued for fourteen days, soaking the dry fields, filling Town Brook almost to overflowing, and turning the rutted street into a sea of slippery mud. Watching the children slide and giggle in the muck, Bradford smiled. Mud was a small price to pay for God's answer to their prayers.

*Faith is taking prayer seriously, knowing God hears
our prayers and will answer.*

FROM GOD'S WORD:
If you believe, you will get anything you ask for in prayer (Matthew 21:22).

LET'S TALK ABOUT IT:
1. Why do you think Elder Brewster suggested a whole day of fasting and prayer?
2. As governor, how did Bradford's decision to set aside a day for prayer and fasting show faith?
3. When you have an important need, do you spend more time worrying about it or praying about it? Why?

BROTHER ANDREW

God's Smuggler

He has a last name—a good Dutch family name. But when he began visiting Christians in Communist countries where, for safety's sake, most believers called each other by their first names only, he, too, began referring to himself simply as "Brother Andrew."

Andrew grew up in Holland in the years between the two world wars. The sleepy village where his father was the blacksmith didn't provide much adventure for this imaginative boy, so he often created his own "adventure"—or mischief. But when the German soldiers rolled into town in 1940, his mischief now had the thrill of patriotic resistance: sugar in the soldiers' gas tanks and firecrackers outside their headquarters.

Andrew was sixteen when Holland was liberated from the Germans in 1944. Most people were sick of war, but Andrew joined the Dutch army and was shipped to the East Indies to put down the rebellion against Dutch colonization. This would certainly provide the adventure he longed for!

But war was not glorious, as he'd imagined. These were real people he was being trained to kill—people who wanted to rule their own country, just as Holland wanted to be independent. When he wasn't fighting, he got drunk so he wouldn't have to think, and when he was fighting, he wore a bright yellow straw hat, daring the "enemy" to shoot him and end his misery.

He did get shot—in the ankle. Recovering in a hospital bed, he began to read the Bible from cover to cover. Crippled and confused about life, he attended a tent revival, then found a church to attend every night of the week. Finally one night he prayed, "Lord, if You will show me the way, I will follow You."

Following Jesus soon came to mean one thing for Andrew: God wanted him to be a missionary. But he needed training. While taking a two-year course with the World Evangelization Crusade (WEC) in Glasgow, Scotland, he came face-to-face with his destiny: In the year 1955, atheistic communism was closing country after country to religious freedom. The West could not forget the believers behind this Iron Curtain! He believed God was calling him to travel to these countries to encourage and help the believers.

What he found on his visits astounded him: Even pastors of churches often did not have Bibles. So the next time Andrew visited, he brought Bibles, smuggling them past the border checkpoints and giving them to the struggling churches. Adventure? Andrew found more than he had ever counted on!

At first he was all alone in this ministry. Then God gave him a wife, Corrie, and finally more partners in ministry. The work in Europe eventually expanded to include China, Cuba, and later Africa, and became known as Open Doors International.

OBEDIENCE
Revival in a Chocolate Factory

~~~~~~~~~~~~~~~~~~~~~~~~~~~~~~~~~~

atcalls and whistles from the factory girls greeted Andrew as he limped into a huge workroom his first day on the job at Ringers' Chocolate Factory in Alkmaar, Holland. It was his first job after returning from the war in the East Indies, and he was determined to make it work. But it wasn't the pain in his injured ankle that bothered him the most; it was the dirty language that peppered him all day long.

"Oh, Lord, how am I supposed to be a missionary here?" he prayed. "These rough girls will never listen." He had recently become a Christian and felt that God was calling him to be a missionary. But if he couldn't tell his co-workers about Jesus, how could he go into the world and do it?

The leader of the filthy talk was a girl named Greetje. Day after day she told dirty stories and egged the other girls on. Only one girl was different.

"Don't mind them too much, Andrew," Corrie said. "Most of them are lonely, and this is the only way they know how to make friends." Andrew was surprised at Corrie's kind heart for these rough girls—until he learned that she was a Christian, too.

After that, as Andrew wheeled his cart up and down the conveyer belt, he kept his eyes and ears open for anyone who seemed to have a problem.

Then he'd tell Corrie, who would talk to the girl in private. Several responded, and soon Corrie and Andrew were taking a small group from the factory to youth meetings in a nearby town.

One morning when Andrew arrived at work, he heard Greetje loudly teasing a blind girl who had been going with them to the youth meetings. "Did you have a good time with Andrew last weekend, Amy? What's he like? Or are all men alike when you can't see them?" Amy was in tears.

Each morning on his way to work, Andrew prayed that God would tell him what to say to people. This morning, the words God put in his mind startled Andrew, but he obeyed anyway. "Shut up, Greetje!" he shouted. "And shut up for good!"

Greetje was so startled, her mouth fell open.

Andrew pursued his advantage. "The bus for the youth meetings leaves at nine o'clock Saturday morning," he shouted across the big room. "Be on it!"

No one was more surprised than Andrew when Greetje climbed on the bus on Saturday. But at the meetings she looked bored and kept to herself.

When the bus got back to Alkmaar, Andrew felt God prompting him to give Greetje a ride home on his bicycle. *This will be a wonderful opportunity to confront her about her sins and her need to be saved*, he thought eagerly. But to his surprise, God seemed to tell him that he should say nothing at all about spiritual things. So Andrew just chatted about the blooming tulip fields they were passing.

The next Monday at work, Greetje was strangely quiet. At lunchtime, she came over and sat beside Andrew. "Know what I thought, Andy?" she said. "I was sure you'd pressure me into 'making a decision for Christ' on that bicycle ride home. I wasn't going to listen. But when you didn't say anything, I began to wonder if you thought I was too sinful to be saved. That got me worried. Maybe God wouldn't listen to me if I said I was sorry. I had to know! So I asked God to forgive my sins and let me start all over again. And I meant it. I cried all night . . . but now I feel great!"

Andrew was astonished. Overnight Greetje was a changed person.

When she stopped telling dirty stories, many of the other girls did, too. She organized a prayer group. When anyone in the factory had problems at home, Greetje organized the others to give help, whether it was clothes or food or money.

Now Andrew knew beyond a shadow of a doubt that it was important to listen to God's voice and obey it.

Obedience is learning to listen for God's voice and doing what He says.

FROM GOD'S WORD:
"[Even if] you are arrested and judged, don't worry ahead of time about what you should say. Say whatever is given you to say at that time, because it will not really be you speaking; it will be the Holy Spirit" (Mark 13:11).

LET'S TALK ABOUT IT:
1. Saying "Shut up!" is not usually considered polite. Do you think Andrew was being obedient to God when he said, "Shut up!" to Greetje? Why?
2. What incident in this story shows that being obedient to God sometimes means not doing or saying something?
3. What do you think would happen if you prayed Andrew's prayer—that God would help you know what to say to people and how to tell them about Jesus—each morning?

TRUST
Game of the Royal Way

he purpose of our training," said the director of the World Evangelization Crusade, "is to teach our students that they can trust God to do what He has said He would do." Andrew nodded. He had seen the words over the archway when he arrived at the WEC school in Glasgow, Scotland: "Have Faith in God."

"Do you have the fees for your first semester's room and board?"

Andrew nodded and laid down the thirty pounds. He had scrimped and saved for that thirty pounds. But how would he get another thirty pounds for the second semester? This would be his first experiment in trusting God for his material needs. "Lord," he prayed, "if this is where you want me to be and what you want me to do, I ask you to supply the rest of my fees. If I am so much as a day late in paying them, I will know I am supposed to go back to the chocolate factory."

During the semester, all the students were sent out on "missionary tours" through Scotland. Each student was given a one-pound note—which he or she had to pay back at the end of the four-week tour. The rules were simple: They were not allowed to take up collections or mention their material needs to anyone. It was an exercise in trusting the

Lord to meet their needs.

"Well, it's theologically sound," said Andrew's friend Kees. "Jesus sent His disciples on a missionary journey without any money or food or extra clothes."

Andrew's team of five young men made an additional promise to the Lord: They would tithe whatever the Lord provided. And somehow the Lord always provided just what they needed; no more, no less. They were invited into homes for a night or a meal; a church where they spoke would send them a check ("even though you don't need money, or you would have mentioned it"); someone would receive a letter from home. Once, after the group boldly invited some young people to come back for "tea" the next day, even though they had nothing to feed them, a package arrived addressed to Andrew just minutes before the students arrived—with a cake from some English friends.

When the team arrived back at the school, they had ten pounds: five to repay the one-pound loans, and five to send to WEC missionaries. After these experiences, Andrew wasn't too surprised to also find a letter waiting for him from friends back home in Holland—with thirty pounds enclosed. Exactly what he needed to pay his second-semester fees.

Andrew became excited about how God was going to meet his next need. It was like a game. He made a move of trust, then it was up to God to make the next move. He called it "the Game of the Royal Way." One day he ran out of laundry soap. Searching his pockets, all he came up with was sixpence. Soap cost eightpence. In faith he set out for the store. There was a sign on the store window: "Sale on laundry soap! Twopence off!" Andrew walked back to school whistling, the box of soap under his arm.

It was important for Andrew to learn how to trust God in the Game of the Royal Way. He was going to need to trust God every step of the way in the ministry God had prepared for him.

*Trust in God's provision means doing what God
wants you to do, even when you don't know
how your needs will be met.*

FROM GOD'S WORD:

"Don't worry about the food or drink you need to live,
or about the clothes you need for your body. . . . The
thing you should want most is God's kingdom and
doing what God wants. Then all these other things you
need will be given to you" (Matthew 6:25, 33).

LET'S TALK ABOUT IT:

1. Why do you think the WEC students were not
   allowed to mention their material needs to anyone?
2. According to Matthew 6:33, what is the most important
   condition for playing the Game of the Royal Way?
3. Do you have a special need right now that is causing
   you worry? Trust God in prayer to meet that need.

ENCOURAGEMENT
"Make the Seeing Eyes Blind"

~~~~~~~~~~~~~~~~~~~~~~~~~~~~~~

Andrew crept quietly to the dormitory door and slipped out into the cool morning air. For a week he had been following the daily agenda of his tour group in Warsaw, Poland, where thousands of youth from around the world had gathered for a Youth Festival. On his application he had said he wanted to exchange ideas: They could tell him about communism, and he would tell them about Christianity.

But today was Sunday. He wanted to go to church—if he could find one. He didn't dare ask his tour guide for directions; the youth festival attendees were supposed to take part in a demonstration at the stadium. Slipping out early, he hailed a taxi and explained where he wanted to go by folding his hands and pretending to pray. Nodding his head, the taxi driver let him off in front of a Reformed church. Yes, he was told by the church members, they had freedom of religion—as long as they avoided politics and didn't criticize the government.

That evening Andrew attended a small Baptist church with very few young people. The people were poorly dressed. But they immediately invited him to speak to them through an interpreter who spoke German. It was Andrew's first sermon behind the Iron Curtain. Afterward the pastor said, "Thank you, just for being here. Sometimes we feel all alone in our struggle. It's good to know the Christians in the West haven't forgotten us."

Those words haunted Andrew. *"We feel all alone. . . ."* He made up his mind. As long as he could find a way to slip through the door, he would go behind the Iron Curtain and encourage the believers there in any way he could.

Again Andrew arranged to go with a tour group to see the "wonders" of communism, this time to Czechoslovakia. Again he managed to slip off to visit several churches. It was too risky to ask a foreigner to speak, but he could bring "greetings" from the church in Holland. "And then if you'd like," one pastor said slyly, "you can bring 'greetings' from Jesus Christ." Once, after his tour guide learned he had been making "private excursions," Andrew was told angrily he was no longer welcome in Czechoslovakia.

In Yugoslavia the churches were open, but the children were being taught in school that only foolish people believed those myths. Still, everywhere he went, people seemed hungry to hear the Word preached. At one service he gave an invitation of commitment, and the entire congregation stood up! Astonished at this eagerness, Andrew outlined a plan of discipleship that included prayer and Bible reading. At this the congregation hung their heads. There were only seven Bibles in the whole congregation.

How could believers grow without the Word of God? Now Andrew's mission grew even clearer. He would bring Bibles to any churches that needed them. Only one problem: It was illegal to bring Bibles into these countries.

On his next trip to Yugoslavia, Andrew had Bibles tucked in every nook and cranny of his suitcases and his little blue Volkswagen. "Lord," he prayed as the line of cars crept closer to the border crossing, "when You were on earth You made blind eyes see. Now I pray that You will make seeing eyes blind. Do not let those guards see anything You don't want them to see."

"Do you have anything to declare?" the border guard growled.

"Well, I have my wristwatch and wallet and a camera. . . ."

"Anything else?"

"Only some small things."

The guard shrugged and waved him through.

Again and again Andrew smuggled Bibles across the borders of Albania, Yugoslavia, Czechoslovakia, and Russia as God made "seeing eyes blind." What joy and encouragement the people felt as they read God's Word for themselves in their own language.

Discouraged people are encouraged when we give them ourselves and the Word of God.

FROM GOD'S WORD:

So encourage each other and give each other strength, just as you are doing now (1 Thessalonians 5:11).

LET'S TALK ABOUT IT:

1. Why did the believers in communist Poland feel so encouraged simply by Andrew's coming to visit them?
2. What else did Andrew do to encourage believers in communist countries?
3. Can you think of a way to encourage someone today who is feeling alone or afraid?

GEORGE WASHINGTON CARVER

The Man Who Saved the South From Poverty

In the fall of 1861, bushwhackers kidnapped a slave girl and her baby from a small Missouri farm, intending to resell them in the South. But Moses Carver, who had bought the girl as a companion for his wife, offered a $300 racehorse for their return. A bounty hunter went after them, but all he had to show for his efforts when he returned was the sickly infant. Carver gave him the racehorse anyway.

The lad was called George, and when the Emancipation Proclamation freed all slaves, he was raised as a member of the Carver family. Too frail for heavy farm work, he developed a deep love for all growing things. He also had a great desire to learn: Why did the roses grow here but not there? Why did the field crops produce less this year than the year before? He desperately wanted to learn to read, but the local white school wouldn't enroll colored children.

Determined to get an education, he left home at age fourteen, working odd jobs to support himself and going to school anywhere that would take him. George Carver wasted little time on bitterness even though racism threw cruel obstacles in his path again and again. Later in life he said, "If I used my energy to right every wrong done to me, I would have no energy left for my work." Eventually he received his master's degree in agriculture and bacterial botany from Iowa State College of Agriculture and Mechanic Arts, and two honorary doctorates.

Carver's thirst to understand God's created world knew no bounds. But why had God given him the skills to unlock nature's secrets? In 1896 he received a letter from Booker T. Washington from Tuskegee Institute in Alabama: Would he come and teach his people how to grow food? The only thing most Southerners knew how to grow was cotton—"King Cotton" they called it. But each year the cotton fields produced less and less. Add years of slavery, the ravages of the Civil War, and the injustices of racism, and most black Americans lived in grinding poverty. Suddenly he knew: God had revealed His plan for George Carver.

For the rest of his life, Dr. Carver dedicated his knowledge of science to helping the common man make a living. He developed two hundred new products from the peanut and 118 practical products from the sweet potato. In so doing, he broke King Cotton's grip on the South, renewing the tired soil and benefiting whites and blacks alike.

The humblest of men, he turned down many well-paying job offers and refused to take a raise in salary. When he died in 1943, he was still receiving the same $125 a week he had started with over forty years earlier. His epitaph reads: "He could have added fortune to fame, but caring for neither, he found happiness and honor in helping the world."

PERSEVERANCE
"Be Like Libby"

George Carver's eyes widened as he untied the paper wrapping and took out the worn brown leather Bible. "A Christmas present for me?" he said in surprise.

"For when you learn to read," said the kindly midwife. Mariah Watkins had seen the fourteen-year-old boy sitting on her fence earlier that fall of 1875, looking hungry and lost. He'd walked to Neosha, Missouri, to attend the Lincoln School for Colored Children—but he had no money or a place to live. The Watkinses had taken him in and were amazed at how hard he worked for his keep. This boy had promise.

"Do you know how to read, Aunt Mariah?" George asked.

Mariah's eyes got misty. "Before the Civil War, I was a slave, just like your mammy. Of all the slaves on the plantation, only one, a woman named Libby, knew how to read. If our master had found out, she probably would've been sold downriver to the South quick as a blink because any slave who had some learnin' was considered uppity and dangerous. But Libby refused to keep this gift to herself and secretly taught some of the rest of us how to read." Mariah took the boy by the shoulders. "George, you must learn all you can, then be like Libby. Go out in the world and give your learnin' back to our people. They're starvin' for a little learnin'."

George was eager to learn and began reading the Bible—a daily habit that gave him strength to the end of his life. But he soon learned everything the Neosha teacher could teach him. Hitching a wagon ride to Fort Scott, Kansas, he got a job cooking to earn money for school books. But one day he saw a colored man dragged out of a jail and burned to death by an angry mob. Frightened, he realized it was dangerous to have dark skin in Fort Scott.

Traveling from town to town in the Midwest, doing odd jobs, George finally graduated from high school. He excelled in botany, biology, chemistry, and art—but there was so much more to learn! Hardly daring to hope, he applied to a Presbyterian college in Highland, Kansas. One day the longed-for letter arrived: He had been accepted! That fall he eagerly arrived on campus. But the dean took one look and said, "You didn't tell us you were a Negro. Highland College does not take Negroes."

George was devastated. Was this the end of the road?

A few years later, renewing his courage, he applied to Simpson College and was accepted—only the second black person in the college's history. At his art teacher's urging, he transferred to the Iowa State College of Agriculture and Mechanic Arts to study horticulture—even though he was barred from the student dining room and had to eat with the kitchen staff. He suffered this indignity patiently, telling himself that ignorant people would not keep him from his duty. The school quickly changed its mind when a prominent white woman who admired George's paintings came to visit him and insisted on eating with him in the kitchen.

After obtaining his master's degree, George was offered a job as professor at Iowa State. But in his mind he heard Mariah Watkins' voice saying, "Be like Libby. Give your learnin' back to your people." When a letter from Tuskegee Institute in Alabama arrived, asking Professor Carver to come teach southern blacks new ways to farm, he knew immediately this was the task God had been preparing him for all along.

Perseverance is knowing God's love is more powerful than the obstacles evil people put in our way.

FROM GOD'S WORD:

Can anything separate us from the love Christ has for us? Can troubles or problems or sufferings or hunger or nakedness or danger or violent death? . . . In all these things we have full victory through God who showed his love for us (Romans 8:35, 37).

LET'S TALK ABOUT IT:

1. What were the obstacles George faced that would have made the average person give up the idea of getting an education?
2. How do you think George had the courage to overcome the racism he faced again and again?
3. What obstacles in your life are keeping you from a God-given goal?

RESOURCEFULNESS
Most Weeds Have
a Purpose

"I cannot offer you money, position, or fame," Booker T. Washington had written to George Carver. "I offer you in their place work—hard, hard work—the task of bringing a people from degradation, poverty, and waste to full personhood."

As Dr. Carver, satchel in hand, stood looking at the dreary frame buildings and barren, dusty grounds of the Tuskegee Institute, Washington's words took on grim meaning. The soil was starving, drained of its nutrients by centuries of planting cotton, only cotton. But some things were growing here and there. Curiously, Carver set down his bag and began picking this leafy stalk, then that one, until he had an armful.

"Lad," he called to the boy who had picked him up from the train, "what is the name of this plant?"

"That?" said the boy. "It's a weed."

"They're all weeds." Carver smiled. "But every weed has a name, and most of them have a purpose."

Within a few weeks, Professor Carver had thirteen students and a task: to set up a laboratory to test local soil and find ways to enrich it for farming. Only one hitch; there was no money to buy equipment for a laboratory.

Carver had never let the lack of money stand in his way. God had given him a brain, and he intended to use it. Marching his students to the school dump, he directed them to save everything possible: bottles, cooking pots, jar lids, wire, odd bits of metal, rusty lamps, broken handles. When the dump had been thoroughly searched, they scoured the back alleys of Tuskegee for china dishes, rubber, curtain rods, and flatirons.

"All this may seem to be just junk to you," he told his skeptical students. "But it is only waiting for us to apply our intelligence to it. Let's get to work!"

Under Carver's supervision, the students punched holes in pieces of tin to make strainers to test soil samples; neatly labeled canning jars held an assortment of chemicals; broken bottles were cut down and transformed into beakers; a discarded ink bottle with a cork and a piece of string made do nicely as a Bunsen burner.

Gradually the makeshift laboratory took shape. And a valuable lesson was learned by the Tuskegee students that carried over into later years, when they took their knowledge into the poverty-stricken pockets of the South. Expensive or brand-new equipment was not a requirement for success.

Dr. Carver was never satisfied with only the obvious use of a thing, especially when it came to things in nature. He firmly believed God had provided all that people needed in the created world; God left it to humans to figure out the secrets locked within each plant, animal, or mineral. To many, a peanut was just a snack and not worth growing as a crop. But with Dr. Carver's probing curiosity and scientific knowledge, the peanut produced butter, oil, milk, dye, salve, shaving cream, paper, shampoo, metal polish, stains, adhesives, plastics, wallboard, and more—for a total of three hundred products! It was this variation that provided new markets for southern crops and saved the South from ruin.

Resourcefulness is using our God-given minds to see usefulness in things (or people) that others just throw away.

FROM GOD'S WORD:

My God will use his wonderful riches in Christ Jesus to give you everything you need (Philippians 4:19).

LET'S TALK ABOUT IT:

1. Why do you think Dr. Carver learned to be resourceful?
2. How is resourcefulness a way of being a good steward of God's creation?
3. Look at some things you throw away. How might you make them useful again?

SERVICE
The School on Wheels

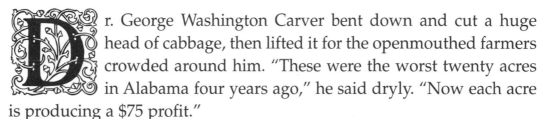r. George Washington Carver bent down and cut a huge head of cabbage, then lifted it for the openmouthed farmers crowded around him. "These were the worst twenty acres in Alabama four years ago," he said dryly. "Now each acre is producing a $75 profit."

It was Farmers' Institute Day at Tuskegee Institute. On the third Tuesday of each month, Dr. Carver talked to local farmers about the importance of rotating their crops and how rotted leaves and kitchen wastes could enrich their soil. "Don't burn off your corn stalks," he scolded. "That's like burning off the outside bills on a roll of dollars. Plow them back into the soil. It's free fertilizer."

As the farmers left, shaking their heads in amazement, Tom Campbell, one of Carver's students, grinned. "Soon as their neighbors see those farmers growing bigger melons than they are, every farmer in Macon County will be hoofin' it up here on third Tuesdays to see your experiment station."

Dr. Carver rubbed his chin thoughtfully. For months he'd been thinking about the dirt-poor farmers tucked away in little hollows all over the county. "No, Tom," he said, "if we want to help the man farthest down take a step up, we're going to have to take the school to them. Say . . . do you think you could scare up a wagon and a horse?"

So it was that the "school man" from Tuskegee and Tom Campbell could be seen each weekend driving the back roads that fall of 1899. It wasn't easy persuading farmers to try something new. "What makes you think you smarter'n me?" scoffed one. "You just as black." Out would come sample plants, and Dr. Carver would patiently explain how they could plant two crops of sweet potatoes a year and feed their hogs with the vines, culls, and peelings—and still do less damage to the soil than one crop of cotton.

"Each plant takes certain things from the soil," he explained. "If you plant only one thing year after year, the soil is soon drained. But chickpeas take nitrogen from the air and put it back into the soil."

"Chickpeas!" snorted a housewife. "What good are chickpeas?" Then Dr. Carver would roll up his sleeves, put a pot of chickpeas on the wood-burning stove, and turn out a tasty meal with mashed chickpeas as the main ingredient in three or four dishes.

Some of Carver's students were doubtful of the school on wheels. "That's no way to make money—giving away free advice."

Carver's eyes flashed fire. "I'm not here to contribute to your own gain," he said, "but to help you lead your people forward. That will be the mark of your success, not the style of clothes you wear, nor the amount of money you put in the bank. It is only service that counts!"

In fact, Carver considered the school on wheels his most important work. He taught backwoods people medical remedies from herbs and plants, how to brighten up their buildings with paints made from color-rich dirt, how to dry fruits and vegetables to feed their families all year long.

And the idea spread. Soon lots of wagons were traveling the back roads. In 1918, the state of Alabama provided a huge motorized truck for the traveling school. Other schools began copying the idea. Educators from foreign countries visited Tuskegee Institute to ask how they could adapt Carver's idea.

When Dr. Carver died in 1943, the chaplain of the school said, "He worshiped God by drawing out of the things that grow goodnesses to serve the needs of mankind."

Service is using God's gifts for the good of others,
not for our own gain.

FROM GOD'S WORD:

Each of you has received a gift to use to serve others. Be good servants of God's various gifts of grace (1 Peter 4:10).

LET'S TALK ABOUT IT:

1. Dr. Carver was a brilliant scientist. He also suffered from prejudice and poverty. Think of several ways he could have become a very rich man.
2. Why do you think he chose to use his gifts to serve other people instead?
3. What gifts do you have (skills, knowledge, etc.) that could lead to "success" in the world? How might you use those gifts serving others?

JONATHAN & ROSALIND GOFORTH

China's "Flaming Preacher"

When young Jonathan Goforth arrived at Knox College in Toronto, Canada, his classmates teased him cruelly. Born February 2, 1859, he had grown up as a poor farm boy. He wore shabby clothes and didn't understand city ways. To improve his appearance at college, he bought some cloth, but before he could get it sewn into new clothes, his fellow students woke him up in the middle of the night. They tied it around his neck like a cape and made him run up and down the dorm hallway, poking fun at him.

They may have laughed at him then, but before he graduated in 1886, his classmates came to respect him so much that they raised the money to send him to China as a missionary. They had seen his sincerity in preaching at rescue missions in Toronto, visiting prisons, and witnessing door-to-door.

The following year Jonathan met and married Rosalind Bell Smith, an attractive, talented, and well-educated woman who had been born (May 6, 1864) and raised in London in a wealthy English family.

In 1888 the Goforths sailed for China, where Jonathan found the Chinese language very difficult to learn as they attempted to adjust to a new culture. Over the years, they had eleven children, only to suffer the sorrow of seeing five of them die very young.

A powerful evangelist, Jonathan became known as the "flaming preacher," sometimes speaking to as many as twenty-five thousand at a time. But the Goforths also used what they called "open-house" evangelism. The Chinese people were curious about how they lived, especially some of their furnishings like a kitchen stove, a sewing machine, and an organ. So they arranged tours of their house all day long. Before they would take a group of fifty people through the house, Rosalind would preach to the women, and Jonathan would preach to the men.

By 1900 an organized revolt known as the Boxer Rebellion had spread throughout China. Its purpose was to drive all foreigners from the country. The Chinese empress encouraged it because Japanese and Western outsiders seemed to be taking over the country. Thousands of foreigners were killed, and the Goforths fled a thousand miles across China to escape. On the way, an angry crowd of men attacked Jonathan and nearly beat him to death with a sword.

When they returned to China about a year later, their approach changed to a traveling evangelistic ministry that produced more than thirteen thousand converts between 1908 and 1913 alone.

The Goforths worked in China for forty-six years before poor health forced them to return to Canada in 1934. In addition to their many converts, they trained sixty-one full-time Chinese evangelists and Bible teachers and established thirty mission stations.

Jonathan died on October 8, 1936, and Rosalind joined him in heaven on May 31, 1942.

TRUST
God Must Come First

he news finally reached Canada where Jonathan Goforth and his wife had taken refuge: The violent Boxer Rebellion in China was finally over. Rosalind looked at her husband expectantly. "Does this mean—?"

"Yes," he said, his face bright with joy. "We can return to China now."

Jonathan went first, and Rosalind followed later with their five children. Paul, the oldest, was eleven. Baby Constance was just eight months. When Rosalind and the children arrived in Shanghai, a telegram was waiting saying Jonathan couldn't meet them. He was in Changte, ill with typhoid fever.

Four Goforth children had already died in China, and Rosalind wasn't about to take any chances with the others, so she waited. A week went by with no word from her husband. Wondering what to do, she traveled up the coast, where she left Paul and Helen, her two eldest, at boarding school in Chefoo and waited some more. A month passed; still no word from Jonathan.

Finally a weak, thin man arrived at her door. At first, Rosalind hardly recognized her husband, but it was Jonathan, and he was alive! All the anxiety of the past few weeks melted away in their joyful reunion.

"Guess what?" Jonathan said eagerly as he began to get his strength back. "The mission board has assigned me the whole region north of Changte, and God has given me a plan for developing it. We'll travel from town to town, renting a building in each place for a month. You can live there and preach to the women during the day while I go out with a team to evangelize the surrounding area. Each night we'll have a meeting back in the building. You can play the organ, and we'll sing plenty of gospel hymns. At the end of a month, we'll leave an evangelist there and move on to a new town."

"But what about the children?" Rosalind said in horror. "We can't drag them all over the country with never a chance to make a good home. Those places will be cold and dirty, the very thing that brings disease. Jonathan, look at you. You yourself almost died from typhoid. We cannot lose another child."

Nevertheless, the day after they arrived back in Changte, little Wallace—not yet three years old—became very ill. For two weeks they didn't know if he'd live or die. When he finally recovered, Jonathan packed to go on his first tour. "Come with me, Rose," he begged. "We must put God first and trust *Him* to protect our children." But she would not come.

The day after he left, baby Constance came down sick—much worse than Wallace had been. Jonathan hurried back, but the baby had already lost consciousness.

As they knelt around Constance's bedside, Rosalind suddenly realized that in putting her children first, she was trying to do God's job of protecting them. Later, after baby Constance had died, she said, "One thing only seemed plain, that I must follow where God should lead. I saw at last that God must come first."

Jonathan reassured her. "I am . . . sure this is God's plan, Rose. . . .The greatest protection is in His will. God can and will keep the children if we trust Him and step out in faith."

Rosalind bowed her head and with great peace said, "O God . . . I will trust You. I will go where You want me to go. I now know that following

Your lead is the safest place for my children."

In the years that followed, their remaining children were never so healthy as when they were traveling and staying in those horrible, temporary homes. In fact, on one occasion, without her mother realizing it, little Mary played all day with another child who had smallpox, but Mary did not contract the deadly disease.

Trusting God includes knowing that we are safest when
we are doing what He wants us to do.

FROM GOD'S WORD:
The LORD replied, "My Presence will go with you, and I will give you rest." Then Moses said to him, "If your Presence does not go with us, do not send us up from here" (Exodus 33:14–15, NIV).

LET'S TALK ABOUT IT:
1. Why was Rosalind so afraid of going on the missions tour?
2. What did Rosalind learn about where the safest place is?
3. What do you think is the difference between doing something foolish and trusting God to take care of you?

VISION

A Tent for Seven Hundred People

he young man cleared his throat nervously. He had heard so much about the Goforths; how could he ever hope to fill their shoes? But the Goforths were now devoting their evangelistic efforts in the north region of China, leaving Changte without a missionary for several years—until now. Uncertain what to do, the new missionary met with Jonathan Goforth to ask his advice. "How do I begin? Won't you help me get started?"

"I would be delighted," said Mr. Goforth. "But in order to do anything in this city now, you will have to do something extraordinary!"

"What do you mean?" the young missionary asked. "Why must I do something extraordinary?"

"Well," said Jonathan, "the little street chapel has become broken down. Only a few believers worship there, and no one pays them any attention. So something unusual must be done to get people interested."

"What do you propose?" asked the young man.

Jonathan thought for a few moments and then answered. "See if you can rent a large, vacant lot near the center of the city. Then put up a huge tent, one that can seat at least seven hundred people. Then start having public meetings—morning, noon, and night—for at least a month."

The young missionary set out to do just as he had been told. But when he asked the mission board for extra money to rent the lot and the tent, the board said, "If you can't fill the little chapel, why should we spend money for some big tent? Goforth must be crazy!"

Discouraged, the young missionary brought the sad news back to Goforth.

"Don't worry," said Jonathan. "A kind woman in Australia has just sent me some extra money to use however I please. We'll use part of that money for these special meetings."

"Would you be our speaker?" asked the young missionary hopefully.

At first Jonathan hesitated. He needed to spend his time finding a Chinese Christian whom he could train to help him with evangelism. But finally he said, "All right. I have a little time right after I get back from Shansi. Have everything ready."

When he got back, the tent was up and the meetings began. The morning and afternoon meetings were for Christians. In the evening, they preached to unbelievers. After a few days, the Spirit of God began to speak to the Christians. They confessed their sins and patched up old disagreements.

Then the unbelievers started responding to the Good News. So many became Christians that a nearby street was renamed "Christian Alley." Soon the tent was too small, and they had to roll up the sides so that those outside could hear. Sometimes there were as many as a thousand waiting to get close enough to hear the Gospel.

On the very last night of the crusade, a man named Mr. Su was riding in his ricksha, a covered, two-sheeled vehicle pulled by a ricksha driver. As he passed the gospel tent on his way to a gambling house, he heard the organ music of Rosalind, the violin of fifteen-year-old Wallace Goforth, and the singing of the Christians. Mr. Su was already quite drunk. "What's that sound?" he demanded of his ricksha driver.

"Those are the Christians," answered his driver. "They have a big tent set up. Haven't you heard about them?"

"No," said Mr. Su. "Take me there."

That night he heard the Gospel for the first time and gave his heart to the Lord. Mr. Su became the Goforth's most faithful co-worker and an excellent Chinese evangelist.

Vision: When we attempt great things for God, we may expect great things from God.

FROM GOD'S WORD:

Make your tent bigger; stretch it out and make it wider. Do not hold back (Isaiah 54:2a).

LET'S TALK ABOUT IT:

1. Why did the mission board not want to give the young, new missionary the money to rent the vacant lot and the big tent?
2. How did God meet Jonathan Goforth's need to find a helper?
3. Tell about a time when you thought God wanted you to do something that seemed too big.

FORGIVENESS
The Impossible Letter

ife on the mission field can be hard. And one of the hardest parts is working out relationships with other missionaries. Living together and sharing gives many opportunities for offending one another.

This was true for Rosalind Goforth. Another missionary hurt her feelings so deeply that for years she would not even speak to him. Then he went to a different mission station, but she still couldn't forgive him. Her hatred was her secret. She wouldn't tell anyone about her feelings.

During this time, Jonathan's ministry was growing, and Rosalind was eager for the Holy Spirit to fill her life in a similar way. "Oh, Lord," she prayed, "I want to be used by You. I want to lead many people to You. Please give me the power of your Spirit so that I can share the Gospel more effectively."

Then came the still Inner Voice of God's Holy Spirit, saying, "Write to the one who offended you. Ask his forgiveness for the way you have treated him!"

"Oh no, Lord," moaned Rosalind. "It is he who wronged me. Never, never can I forgive him."

But then a second time the Inner Voice whispered, "Write and forgive him."

Again Rosalind protested. "Never. He has done nothing to deserve forgiveness."

When the clear Inner Voice spoke again telling her to write, she jumped up from her prayer and said, "I might as well forget this whole thing. I can never forgive that man."

She found some of her friends who were talking and having a good time, and joined in their laughter to hide how upset she felt.

For several months after that, she preached and prayed in public and carried on so that no one would know that she and God were at a standstill in their relationship. But inside, her heart became harder, colder, and more hopeless.

Then one day she recalled the scene in John Bunyan's book *Pilgrim's Progress* where Christian was talking to a man in a cage. *That's what I feel like*, thought Rosalind. *I feel like I'm in a cage.* In Bunyan's book, the man in the cage explained that God's Spirit had left him because he had saddened the Holy Spirit by not obeying His voice.

That is just like me, thought Rosalind. She found a friend to talk to, and in a few moments she was crying so hard she could barely speak. Soon the whole story came out. "I have saddened the Holy Spirit by not obeying His voice," she said, "and now He has left me!"

"But Mrs. Goforth," said her friend, "are you willing to write that letter?"

"Of course," cried Rosalind. "Now that I know how miserable it is to be out of fellowship with God, I would do anything for another chance."

"Then by all means, go write the letter!" urged her friend. "It is not too late!"

Suddenly, with hope restored, Rosalind jumped up and went into her house and wrote the letter. It was a simple, short apology for her actions and unforgiveness. But what a relief it was to send it off in the mail. Joy and thankfulness returned to her spirit as she realized that she had obeyed God.

Forgiveness is the release that brings back joy and sets the world right again.

FROM GOD'S WORD:

"If you forgive others for their sins, your Father in heaven will also forgive you for your sins. But if you don't forgive others, your Father in heaven will not forgive your sins" (Matthew 6:14–15).

LET'S TALK ABOUT IT:

1. Why was it important for Rosalind to forgive the person who offended her?

2. Why is it important for us to forgive others, even if we don't think they "deserve" it? (See Matthew 6:14–15 above.)

3. Is there someone who has offended or hurt you whom you need to forgive? Ask your heavenly Father to give you the grace to do so.

BILLY
GRAHAM

———— ❦ ————

Evangelist to the World

Billy Graham was born on November 7, 1918, on a dairy farm outside Charlotte, North Carolina. At the age of sixteen, he gave his life to Jesus. After a brief and troublesome time at Bob Jones College in Tennessee, he went on to graduate from Florida Bible Institute in Tampa. During his time there, he felt God calling him to the ministry and began preaching in various churches. Finally he was ordained as a Southern Baptist minister in 1940.

However, he felt he needed additional training and applied to Wheaton College in Illinois. Even though he had already graduated from one college, Billy at first felt out of place in this northern school, but it wasn't long before people discovered his preaching ability. He began to preach at the nearby "Tabernacle" attended by some three hundred local business and professional people, many Wheaton students, and several college professors. It was a scary audience for the twenty-two-year-old preacher, but the church liked him and asked him to be their regular pastor.

While at Wheaton, Billy met Ruth McCue Bell. They were married in 1943 and have since had five children.

After graduating and serving a couple years as a pastor in Western Springs, Illinois, Billy became a full-time evangelist with Youth for Christ. He began traveling throughout the United States and also in Great Britain.

In 1947, he became the president of Northwestern Bible College, a small university in Minnesota. These responsibilities, however, did not fit well with his traveling evangelistic ministry, which he was starting to do with a team of men not under Youth for Christ. In 1950, this team was organized as the Billy Graham Evangelistic Association, and the next year, Billy resigned from his position as president of Northwestern Bible College.

The Los Angeles crusade in 1949 was his first really big evangelistic meeting. Housed in a huge tent, so many well-known celebrities were converted in this crusade that the newspapers began reporting on the meetings. That led to more people coming, and the crusade was extended from a planned three weeks to eight weeks. Billy nearly collapsed from exhaustion.

Over the years, Billy Graham crusades took place in major cities in more than eighty countries where Billy has preached in person to over 110 million people. Thousands and thousands of Christians worldwide mark the occasion of their decision to follow Jesus Christ at one of these crusades.

In addition, he has spoken by radio or television to hundreds of millions of other people through "The Hour of Decision" broadcasts.

Billy Graham's worldwide reputation has earned him frequent invitations to speak with presidents and monarchs, criminals and celebrities, generals and armies all over the world. Some he has supported in their Christian faith. Others, who lack faith in Christ, he challenged to turn to Jesus. But he never fails to present the message of the Gospel for the needs of today.

PURITY
The Modesto Manifesto

A manifesto is a list of rules or plans by which a group agrees to be guided. It is usually issued or printed publicly.

When Billy Graham started having evangelistic crusades that were not part of Youth for Christ, which was an organization with a very good reputation, he knew that many traveling evangelists who went about on their own had bad reputations. Some performed fake miracles. Some begged people for money, making them feel guilty if they did not give more and more. Some were not faithful to their wives.

One afternoon during their 1948 Modesto, California, crusade, Billy Graham called the team together. "I know that none of us want to do these wrong things," he said, "but how can we be sure that no one accuses us of them anyway?" To work on the problem, he sent everyone to their hotel rooms to come up with a list of wrong behaviors they needed to guard against.

Later, when everyone gathered back together, their lists were almost the same! Together the team came up with a list of four commitments that would uphold the Bible's standard of absolute honor and purity.

1. *To not be greedy for money.* Therefore, they decided to avoid doing anything that would make people feel guilty for not giving or suggest that

they could earn God's favor by giving more. In order to downplay the offerings during the crusades, they decided that they would rely as much as possible on money raised by the local planning committee before each crusade. Therefore, they would not have to beg for money during their meetings just to pay the bills.

2. *To be completely faithful to their spouses.* Therefore, the men on the team promised to avoid any situation that might even appear like they were flirting with other women. From that day on, Billy Graham did not travel alone with, meet alone with, or eat alone with any woman other than his wife. This simple but wise rule has protected him from ever being accused of "fooling around" with other women.

3. *To support local churches.* When some traveling evangelists came to town, they spoke against the local church and made the people unhappy with their pastors and leaders. Billy Graham and his team agreed not to criticize local ministers. They desired to cooperate with all who would cooperate with them in spreading the Gospel.

4. *To be truthful in their advertising and reporting.* In order to stir up greater interest, some traveling evangelists claimed to be more successful, draw larger crowds, or make more converts than was true. Some of their advertising would say things like, "Come hear the greatest preacher of the century." Billy Graham did not want to puff himself up. He wanted only to lift up Jesus. So his ads used themes like "Christ for This Crisis" rather than saying how great he or his team was.

Some time after the team made these commitments, Cliff Barrows, one of the team members, began calling it the Modesto Manifesto. It reflected what each team member already believed, but it was reassuring to have committed themselves to it with all their hearts and minds. They were determined that purity and truthfulness would characterize their lives and ministry. And it was good to know that they all felt the same.

Purity in public ministry requires avoiding even the appearance of wrongdoing.

FROM GOD'S WORD:

Test everything. Keep what is good, and stay away from everything that is evil (1 Thessalonians 5:21–22).

LET'S TALK ABOUT IT:

1. Why did some traveling evangelists have bad reputations?
2. Why did Billy Graham decide never to travel alone with, meet alone with, or eat alone with any woman other than his wife?
3. Tell about a situation where you weren't really doing anything wrong yourself, but you got in trouble because you were with someone else who was doing wrong. How might things have been different if you had walked away so it wouldn't have looked like you were involved?

FAITH
Billy's "Hour of Decision"

~~~~~~

Most people don't realize that great men and women of God sometimes face a crisis of faith. Billy Graham was no exception!

At the age of thirty, after preaching the Gospel for over ten years, Billy became confused about the truthworthiness of the Bible. Was it all true, all God's Word, or were parts of it made up by humans? If it was not all true, how was he to be sure which parts he could trust?

Billy's confusion stemmed from a very close old friend, Chuck Templeton. Chuck had resigned his position as pastor of a church in Toronto, Canada, and had enrolled in Princeton Theological Seminary. There Chuck studied some of the new religious thinkers of the day who claimed to be sincere Christians but who changed the meanings of some of the foundations of the faith.

Chuck urged Billy to consider this new way of thinking, particularly as it related to the Bible. "How can you believe it's all true?" asked Chuck. "You know that there are parts that seem to disagree with one another, and other stories—like Noah and the ark or Jonah being swallowed by a fish—are so strange that no thinking person can believe them. You don't have to believe in all that stuff in order to be a Christian. Get with the times, Billy. This is 'enlightened' Christianity!"

Doubts began to creep in as Billy read these new religious thinkers, but he also studied the Bible itself. He considered Paul's words, "All Scripture is given by God" (2 Timothy 3:16), and he knew that in the original Greek, Paul was saying that all Scriptures were "God-breathed writings." Jesus himself had said, "Earth and sky will be destroyed, but the words I have said will never be destroyed" (Matthew 24:35). Billy also noted the many occasions where Jesus considered the Scriptures completely trustworthy, even such stories as Noah and Jonah. There was no question: Either the whole Bible was true, or no one could be sure which parts were true.

Billy was no fool, and he was not the kind of guy to fool himself. He knew that if he couldn't trust the Bible—the whole Bible—he couldn't go on preaching. He might continue as a quiet Christian, but he couldn't be sure that what he was telling others was true. He would have no foundation to really preach to people other than his own ideas.

These struggles became even more real in 1949 after a discouraging crusade in Altoona, Pennsylvania, where there was very little response. Maybe God wasn't in this, after all.

Unable to sleep one moonlit night, he took a walk in the mountains, where he faced his personal "hour of decision." By an old stump, he dropped to his knees and prayed, "O God! There are many things in this book I do not understand. There are many problems with it for which I have no solution." All of that was true, but he knew there was one more thing he needed to confess, and by the power of the Holy Spirit, he finally added, "Nevertheless, Father, I am going to accept it as Your Word—by faith! I will believe that it is Your inspired Word."

Freed from his doubts, the next crusade, in Los Angeles, exceeded all hopes. It was planned for three weeks but extended to eight. Hundreds of thousands heard the Gospel, and thousands accepted Christ as Savior. The following year, Billy started a radio broadcast that he called "The Hour of Decision."

Anyone who tries to have faith without faith
has no true faith at all.

FROM GOD'S WORD:

Then [God] said, "Write this, because these words are true and can be trusted" (Revelation 21:5b).

LET'S TALK ABOUT IT:

1. What caused Billy Graham to start doubting the trustworthiness of the Bible?
2. How did he finally overcome those doubts?
3. What things do you have to believe by faith in order to have a solid faith?

RESISTING EVIL
The Ends Don't
Justify the Means

n an interview for ABC's *Prime Time America* (December 17, 1992), Diane Sawyer asked Billy Graham, "If you could erase one evil from the world, what would it be?"

Billy didn't hesitate a moment. "Race," he said. "If I could make an evil disappear, it would be the evil of racial division."

Billy's strong opinion about the importance of racial reconciliation reflected Billy's concern stemming back to the early days of his crusades. Though he had grown up in the South and had adopted many of the attitudes of that region, his study of the Bible led him to the conclusion that racial prejudice was not only wrong, but Christians especially should demonstrate love toward all peoples.

Billy Graham decided he would not allow racial separation in his crusades no matter where he spoke. When President Bill Clinton was a boy, he asked his Sunday school teacher to drive him fifty miles to hear Billy Graham "because he was a man trying to live by what he said," the president later said. Billy Graham had agreed to hold a crusade in racially troubled Arkansas only if blacks and whites could attend together and sit together.

Billy Graham would go anywhere to share the Gospel with any president, dictator, head of state—good or bad—average person or low-down criminal, but he would not allow his crusades to be occasions for racial unfairness. Some people objected, saying it was more important to "just preach the Gospel." But Billy held firm: The ends don't justify the means.

One day his long-time friend, Dr. Martin Luther King, Jr., gave him this advice: "You stay in the stadiums, Billy, preaching to the people, because you will have far more impact on the white establishment there than you would if you marched in the streets with me."

For twenty-two years Billy Graham had been invited to speak in South Africa, but he always refused because the laws of that country would not permit people of different colors to meet together in the same crowd. But in 1973, South African pastor Michael Cassidy helped get permission for crusades embracing all races and most denominations in the coastal city of Durban and later in Johannesburg, South Africa's largest city.

Durban's King's Park Stadium was packed with forty-five thousand people, half of whom were nonwhites. And the Wanderers Stadium in Johannesburg set a record with sixty thousand. At the end of the crusades, more than seven thousand people had made decisions for Christ.

One South African newspaper declared in its headline, "Apartheid Doomed," meaning that the laws to keep the races apart could not last. It noted that the Billy Graham crusade was the largest multi-racial crowd ever to assemble in South Africa. Even though it was not until 1991 that the government ended all segregation laws, many people point to the Billy Graham crusades of 1973 as one of the steps in resisting this evil and in helping to avoid an all-out civil war.

One cannot truly resist evil while giving in
to it just a little.

FROM GOD'S WORD:

It would be [wrong] to say, "We should do evil so that good will come" (Romans 3:8a).

LET'S TALK ABOUT IT:

1. Why do you think Billy Graham thought it was so important for Christians, especially, to demonstrate love toward people of every color?
2. What effect do you think Billy Graham's decision to not hold a crusade in South Africa unless all races could attend had on the people of color there?
3. Tell about a time when someone tried to get you to do something wrong by telling you, "Come on. It won't hurt just this once." What was the result?

BETTY
GREENE

---❦---

Pioneer Missionary Pilot

On Betty Greene's sixteenth birthday, her father gave her and her twin brother the gift of an airplane ride. Aviation was the new thing with Charles Lindbergh's flight across the Atlantic Ocean in 1927 and Amelia Earhart's flight in 1928. Betty, born on June 24, 1920, in Seattle, followed each event with enthusiasm and saved every penny to take flying lessons for herself.

Her Christian parents supported her interest in aviation, but when it came to college, they encouraged her to enroll in a nursing program at the University of Washington. But Betty was unhappy with that, so she dropped out after two years. Then an elderly Christian woman, who knew of Betty's interest in aviation, suggested that she combine her flying with missionary work. "Of course, dear," she said. "Think of all the time—and sometimes lives—that could be saved if missionaries didn't have to spend weeks hacking their way through jungles."

Suddenly, Betty had a direction for her life. She returned to school to study for missions and continued working toward her pilot's license. When World War II broke out, she signed up as a WASP (a Women's Air Force Service Pilot) to get additional flying experience while serving her country. As a WASP she flew many kinds of planes—from fighters to bombers—from their factories to where they were needed. She also served as a high-altitude test pilot and towed targets for live ammo anti-aircraft gunnery drills.

One day she wrote an article for InterVarsity's HIS magazine about using planes to help missionaries, something that had been done in only a few situations before. When Navy pilot Jim Truxton read the article, he contacted Betty and suggested starting an aviation organization to serve missionaries once the war ended. The Christian Airmen's Missionary Fellowship was officially born on May 20, 1945. Later it changed its name to Missionary Aviation Fellowship (MAF).

Betty, who was released from the service before the other interested pilots, helped set up offices in Los Angeles. After the new organization obtained its first airplane, a red Waco biplane, Betty flew it down to Mexico to help Wycliffe Bible Translators in their jungle training camp. She became MAF's first official pilot.

At age twenty-six, Betty was finally doing what God had prepared her for. And she loved it! The flight into or out of the jungle camp took one hour and forty-five minutes, while hiking through the jungle required ten days to two weeks.

Altogether, she flew more than 4,800 hours, bringing medical supplies and food to missionaries, flying sick and injured people to hospitals, and carrying missionary children to their schools or to be with their parents for vacation. She served in Mexico, Peru, Africa, and Indonesia.

In 1962, she retired from fieldwork but continued to ferry planes for MAF from time to time. Finally, she returned to Seattle for the last years of her life until she died in April 1997.

PREPARATION
Escape of the Duck[1]

The red Waco biplane was coming in a little too fast for the strange airfield in El Real, Mexico, but Betty Greene wanted the new pilot, George Wiggins, to get a feel for the plane. He touched down all right, but the biplane had a large radial engine that made it difficult to see the runway ahead once the tail was on the ground. And at this airport, an unfamiliar pilot could be in trouble if he couldn't see where he was going because the runway was not straight. Halfway down the field, it turned a little bit, and right at the turn was an old shack.

"Watch the shack, George!" Betty cautioned. George cut the corner, but the wings hit the building. Crunch! The plane spun around and came to a shuddering stop.

Betty winced. It wasn't her fault, but this wasn't how she wanted to end her first assignment on the mission field. George Wiggins had come down to replace Betty so she could go to Peru and fly another plane for Cameron Townsend, the founder of Wycliffe Bible Translators[2].

Now Nate Saint[3], MAF's mechanic, would have to spend several

---

[1]*Adapted from the forthcoming book by Betty Greene and Dietrich Buss,* Flying High: The Story of Betty Greene, *Chap. 7.*
[2]*See* Hero Tales II *by Dave and Neta Jackson (Minneapolis: Bethany House Publishers, 1997).*
[3]*See* Fate of the Yellow Woodbee *by Dave and Neta Jackson (Minneapolis: Bethany House Publishers, 1997).*

months in Mexico repairing the Waco before it could fly again.

Once Betty was in Peru, she faced another problem. The plane she was to fly was a Grumman Duck that could land on water or the ground—ideal for the many rivers in the Amazon Basin—but it was trapped in the city of Lima on the west coast. The missionaries who needed it were on the other side of the towering Andes Mountains.

The military man who turned the plane over to MAF looked Betty up and down doubtfully. "No woman can fly this brute," he growled, "much less take it over the mountains."

Betty just smiled. She knew God had prepared her when she had done high-altitude testing during the war. She had had experience flying many different kinds of aircraft as a WASP.

Her first attempt to cross the mountains was blocked by clouds. Three days later the weather looked better, and she and Cameron Townsend took off in the morning. At twelve thousand feet, Betty put on her oxygen mask. Higher and higher they went looking for a gap in the clouds that would let them fly through a canyon. Would the Duck ever escape? At sixteen thousand feet they followed a mountain river up its gorge until they just skimmed over the pass. But ahead, all they could see was a blanket of clouds stretching out to the east. How would they ever get down through the clouds to land at the town of San Ramon?

On Betty flew, praying that if she couldn't find a way down through the clouds, the clouds behind her would not close in to prevent her return back through the pass. Then a hole appeared below her, and she threaded the old Duck down through it where she could fly along for sixty or seventy miles under the clouds but above the plateau. When the plateau dropped away, another layer of clouds lay on the basin floor. Betty hesitated to go much lower until she was certain she could land at San Ramon. If she could not land, she did not want to have to climb all those thousands of feet back up to cross back over the Andes.

Finally Betty sighted San Ramon through a break in the clouds. Gratefully, she circled the Duck through the break to a perfect landing.

Betty Greene grinned at Cameron Townsend. She had just become the first woman pilot to cross the Andes Mountains.

Whatever God takes us through can prepare us for future assignments in His service.

FROM GOD'S WORD:

Just as the heavens are higher than the earth, so are my ways higher than your ways and my thoughts higher than your thoughts (Isaiah 55:9).

LET'S TALK ABOUT IT:

1. After being a passenger in one plane accident (even though no one was hurt), how do you think Betty felt facing a dangerous flight no other woman had ever attempted?
2. Betty Greene had many flight instructors before she flew for MAF, but who really organized her training program? What were some of the things she learned that helped her get over the Andes?
3. How might God use something you are learning to do now at some time in the future?

AVAILABILITY
Come When You're Called[4]

Two-year-old Loraine Conwell giggled as she popped another peanut into her mouth. She was playing on the porch of her house with some other children in the middle of the morning in June 1967. Three days earlier her mother had given birth to a new baby sister, and now Mrs. Conwell was inside resting.

The Conwells were missionaries at the Sudan United Mission leprosarium (a hospital for lepers) in the Nuba Mountains, some two hundred miles northwest of Malakal, Sudan, in Africa, where Betty Greene was stationed with her MAF airplane.

Suddenly, little Loraine began to cough. Then she began to choke and had trouble breathing. Running to her side, Loraine's mother realized that a peanut must have gone down the child's windpipe.

"Turn her upside down and smack her back," instructed one of the nurses as she and Roy Conwell, Loraine's father, came running. But it did no good. They even tried dusting a little pepper in Loraine's nose to make her sneeze, but the peanut wouldn't budge. Fortunately, it was not completely blocking her windpipe, so Loraine could breathe with much

[4]Flying High, *Chap. 14.*

effort and wheezing. But there was also the chance that the peanut might move the wrong way and completely block her windpipe.

Roy Conwell could not stand around watching while his little girl gasped for air any longer. He had to go for help! But the closest telephone was thirty miles away, and in that time of the year—the rainy season—it could take a day or more to travel thirty miles. "I'm going to take the tractor," he said. "It's slow, but there'll be less chance of it getting stuck in the mud."

He got to a phone by seven that evening and immediately phoned the MAF house in Malakal. "Can you come quickly?" he asked Betty Greene. "We have a medical emergency. If I can't get my little girl to the hospital soon, she'll probably die."

By first light the next morning, Betty was on her way. She picked up the child, her father, and a nurse at the leprosarium and flew them 320 miles to the hospital in Khartoum. There a specialist performed a delicate operation to remove the peanut, and little Loraine was on her way to recovery.

But God was watching over little Loraine in other ways that day. The specialist who removed the peanut was scheduled to leave for London the next day. Had Loraine not been brought to the hospital by air, she would have arrived too late to receive that doctor's help, even if she had survived the slow overland trip.

Also, just a few hours after Loraine came out of surgery, a terrible dust storm struck the city of Khartoum. It was so severe that everything turned as dark as midnight. The lights came on, but then the power failed, and everything was brought to a stop.

"Thanks," Roy Conwell said to Betty. "If you hadn't come as soon as possible after I called, the dust storm might have made it impossible for us to land in Khartoum—or the power might have failed while the doctor was trying to operate."

Betty nodded, her own heart swelling with thankfulness. As an MAF pilot, being available was what it was all about.

Availability to the Lord means coming when you are called and going where you are sent.

FROM GOD'S WORD:

Samuel said, "Speak, Lord. I am your servant and I am listening" (1 Samuel 3:10).

LET'S TALK ABOUT IT:

1. How do you think Roy Conwell felt having to drive a slow tractor for seven hours just to get to a telephone?

2. What do you think might have happened if Betty Greene had not responded as soon as possible after she was called for help?

3. Tell about a time when it was important for you to be "available" by doing what you were asked to do right when you were asked to do it?

CAUTION
No Old, Bold Pilots [5]

"Ilu station," Betty Greene spoke into her radio microphone, "this is Papa Tango Foxtrot. Do you read me?" She was flying in the mountains of New Guinea in an MAF Cessna with a partial license number of PTF or, in radio talk, Papa Tango Foxtrot. The clouds had closed in, and she wasn't sure she could make it over the mountains to her stop at Ilu station in the Baliem Valley.

The static hissed in her earphones as she strained to hear a response. She tried again, "Ilu station, this is Papa Tango Foxtrot. Do you read me?"

Then the faint words came through the static. "Roger, Foxtrot. This is Ilu station. Over."

"Ilu, from Papa Tango Foxtrot, I read you weakly. How is your weather? Over."

Betty was on a routine flight from Sentani on the north coast of Irian Jaya to deliver supplies to the Unevangelized Fields Mission in the Bailem Valley on the other side of the mountain range. But there was a thick layer of clouds over the coastal jungle that seemed to be pasted to the mountains. As she had turned west along the range looking for a break in the clouds that would let her cross over into the Bailem Valley, she radioed back to Sentani, telling the control tower what she was doing.

[5]*Ibid., Chap. 16*

Now she was checking with the people in Bailem Valley to see if the weather was clear there. Betty was licensed to fly by instruments, so legally she could have flown up into the clouds, over the mountains, and down into the valley. But that would have been reckless not knowing what the weather was like on the other side.

"Papa Tango Foxtrot" came the scratchy voice over the radio, "our valley has [mumble, mumble]. Over."

"Say again, Ilu," said Betty.

"Roger, Papa Tango Foxtrot. We have low clouds. I say again, low clouds. Over."

"Are there any breaks?" asked Betty.

"Negative, Papa Tango Foxtrot. No breaks."

"Roger that, Ilu," said Betty. "I'm north of the range with solid cloud cover. No chance to get through, so I am returning to Sentani. I will try again tomorrow. Papa Tango Foxtrot, out."

It had always been Betty's practice—as well as MAF policy—not to take needless risks. Caution was the way to keep alive to fly another day.

The next day the weather cleared, and she was able to land in Ilu with no problem.

However, a few years later another MAF pilot was trying to get into the Baliem Valley during poor weather. He was flying in from the south coast and thought he could follow the river all the way, even though the clouds were very low. It, too, was a risky venture, but he pushed on. In the poor visibility, he followed the wrong river. Soon the river valley became a narrow canyon and then a gorge, and he did not have enough room to turn around. He crashed into the trees and burned, killing himself and his passengers.

Among pilots there's a saying: "There are old pilots, and there are bold pilots. But there are no old, bold pilots!" It means that in flying—as in life—if we do not learn to practice caution, our foolishness will catch up with us and result in tragedy.

*God expects us to use caution and practice safety
so we can serve Him longer.*

FROM GOD'S WORD:

The [cautious] see danger ahead and avoid it, but fools keep going and get into trouble (Proverbs 27:12).

LET'S TALK ABOUT IT:

1. Why didn't Betty Greene use instruments to fly up into the clouds and over the mountains?
2. Why do you think the other MAF pilot decided to keep flying into the Baliem Valley even though visibility was poor? What was the result?
3. What do you think is the difference between caution and fear? Give an example of each.

CLARENCE JONES

Mr. Missionary Radio

Clarence Wesley Jones was born December 15, 1900, to parents who were officers in the Salvation Army. At the age of twelve, Clarence begged his parents to let him join the Salvation Army band on the streets of Chicago. After trying out all the instruments, he chose the trombone and made music enthusiastically to the praise of God.

Clarence was a natural musician. While still a teenager, he was invited to join the band at Moody Church. As he listened to the dynamic preaching of Moody's pastor, Paul Rader, Clarence realized that growing up in a devout Christian family didn't equal salvation. On October 27, 1918, he made a personal commitment to Jesus Christ. He immediately enrolled at Moody Bible Institute to prepare himself for ministry.

In 1922, Paul Rader left Moody and established the Chicago Gospel Tabernacle, holding evangelistic meetings every night of the week. After graduation, Clarence came on staff at the "Tab," as it was called, playing his trombone in the band, leading singing, setting up chairs, preaching, organizing a boys club (the beginning of AWANA clubs)—whatever had to be done. When Rader got excited about using radio to help spread the Gospel, Clarence got excited, too, eventually directing the

Tabernacle radio broadcasts. For a young man in his twenties, it was invaluable training in leadership and ministry.

In 1924 Clarence married Katherine Welty, whom he had met on an evangelistic tour. Several years later, at the "Tab's" summer campground, Clarence responded to a missions challenge, feeling the call of God to take radio and its potential for spreading the Gospel to South America. Even though most people thought it was a crazy idea, Clarence persisted—traveling to South America to explore possible sites, getting more education, linking up with experienced missionaries, establishing a new mission organization (World Radio Missionary Fellowship), raising funds. On Christmas Day, 1931, HCJB—the Voice of the Andes— broadcast its first program from Quito, Ecuador, to a handful of listeners. Katherine and their three children (a fourth was born in Ecuador, and two died in infancy) joined Clarence and the tiny HCJB staff a few months later.

During these early years, Clarence was basically in charge of both programming and operations. He always expected excellence, from himself and others. Always on time, energetic, and brimming with ideas, he never sat back and rested on what had already been done, but always looked forward to what could be done next. Within ten years, HCJB was broadcasting radio programs in many different languages, twenty-four hours a day, around the world.

In spite of several personal tragedies, Clarence never lost his vision for reaching the world with the Gospel. He and Katherine visited many countries to encourage others involved in missionary radio—and was always ready to play that trombone. In 1975, he was the first person to be inducted into the Religious Broadcasters Hall of Fame. At the time of his death in 1986, Clarence Wesley ("C.W.") Jones had earned his nickname, "Mr. Missionary Radio."

VISION
"Jones' Folly"

larence Jones watched the skyline of New York grow larger as his ship steamed into the harbor. He felt a little foolish coming home after his trip to South America. "God is calling me to set up a missionary radio station," he had announced to his family and friends. But every country he'd visited in 1926—Venezuela, Columbia, Panama, Cuba—had refused to give an "evangelical" a radio permit.

He remembered the day Paul Rader, the pastor of the Gospel Tabernacle where Clarence played trombone in the band, had announced to the staff, "The mayor of Chicago just called! He wants us to do a program for Chicago's first radio station. At last we're going to fight Satan in his own territory—the air!"

Radio! Some Christians called it "the devil's toolbox." But Clarence quickly saw its potential to take the Gospel into the homes of people who might never step inside a church. The young man learned everything he could about radio, from announcing to directing to producing programs. If radio could multiply the number of people who heard the Gospel in Chicago, what about places that had never heard about Jesus?

In South America, after riding horseback for days on steep mountain trails to get to remote tribes, he had felt even stronger about radio's potential to reach people in remote areas with the Gospel. But all the doors seemed to be closed. Had he heard the Lord wrong?

Back home in Chicago, Clarence and Katherine met two missionary couples home on furlough from Ecuador. Both the Clarks and the Larsons became excited about Clarence's vision for radio. "We have a very good relationship with the Ecuadoran government," they said. "We'll help you get a permit." The Joneses were elated.

But the missionaries admitted there were only six radio receivers in the whole country. To make matters worse, two American engineers told him, "Ecuador is probably the worst place in the world for a radio station. The high mineral content in the Andes Mountains will scramble your signal. Stay away from the mountains." The U.S. State Department advised, "Get away from the equator. We suggest you avoid Ecuador altogether." Avoid Ecuador? The staff at the Gospel Tabernacle began whispering about "Jones' Folly."

But Clarence was sure God wanted a radio station in South America. And doors were opening! The Ecuadoran government granted a twenty-five-year permit. Two businessmen in Quito agreed to sell radio receivers to people. And his missionary friends had found a small plot of land to build the station. "The more obstacles you have, the more opportunity there is for God to do something," Clarence decided. The Larsons and Clarks agreed.

Within ten years, the 250-watt station in Quito grew to 10,000 watts. Letters were coming in from all over the world: South America, Japan, Sweden, New Zealand, India, Russia. Clarence and the HCJB staff were astonished. Normally a 10,000-watt station couldn't broadcast so far.

At an international meeting of radio technicians, an HCJB staff member was complimented, "What a smart operation! The equator is the very finest location for north-south broadcasting. With equal distance from the magnetic poles, it's the one place in the world freest from atmospheric disturbance. And with your hundred-foot antenna sitting on a ninety-six-hundred-foot mountain, you virtually have a ten-thousand-foot antenna. The higher above sea level you can get your tower, the farther the signal will travel. Amazing how your engineers have chosen the best site on earth!"

When Clarence heard this he laughed. "God knew it all along!"

Vision is catching a glimpse of God's worldwide plan.

FROM GOD'S WORD:

" 'Call to Me, and I will answer you, and show you great and mighty things, which you do not know' " (Jeremiah 33:3, NKJV).

LET'S TALK ABOUT IT:

1. Why do you think Clarence Jones was convinced it was important to build a missionary radio station in South America?

2. Jeremiah 33:3 was Clarence Jones' favorite verse. How do you think this verse helped him deal with obstacles?

3. How do you think catching a vision of "God's big plan" could help you deal with obstacles or problems in your life?

OBEDIENCE
The Piece of Junk

The black panel truck with HCJB painted on the side rolled to a stop in the mountain village. Men, women, and children in colorful blankets and straw hats crowded around the "Radio Rodante." Big smiles lit up on brown faces as Spanish music blared from the speakers mounted on top of the truck. Then a scratchy voice preached a gospel message in the Quechua language.

"This is a fantastic way to introduce people to radio," said Clarence Jones to Reuben Larson, his friend and co-worker, as the radio truck lurched over the rutted road to the next village. "But what about the villages that have no roads? And how can we reach people who are too poor to buy a radio set?"

The men began brainstorming how to build a simple radio receiver a whole village could use. Soon HCJB staff members had set up fifty different "Listening Posts" around Ecuador with radio receivers pre-tuned to HCJB. In one town, a cotton mill worker gathered all the children of the village into his home once a week to listen to "Sunday School of the Air." In another, sixty-five neighbors crowded into the tailor's house to listen to gospel programs on the radio.

The Gospel was going out on the airwaves all over Central and South

America. But with only a 1,250-watt station, how could they reach "the uttermost parts of the earth"? Then in 1938 HCJB heard about a used 5,000-watt transmitter available for $10,000 in Chicago. The mission trustees agreed Clarence should go back to the States and take a look at it. "If you can raise the money, go ahead and buy it," they said.

The Jones family went home for their first furlough, but at the end of the year, Clarence had raised only $3,000. During a visit to R.G. LeTourneau, a wealthy businessman, LeTourneau said, "I'd like you to build a radio station in the Philippines. I'll finance the whole operation." Clarence was stunned. Maybe this was God's way of reaching the whole world with gospel radio.

But a still, small voice said in his heart, "Stay with Ecuador."

"I'm sorry, sir, but God has called me to South America. You'll have to find someone else for the Philippines." And Clarence turned to go.

"Well, then," said LeTourneau, "I'd like to help you get that 5,000-watt transmitter." And he handed Clarence a check for $7,000—the exact amount still needed.

Elated, Clarence headed for Chicago and was just about to sign the papers for the transmitter when he again heard that still, small voice saying, "Wait." What? The trustees would think he was crazy if he let this opportunity go!

But Clarence said, "I can't buy this right now. I'll be in touch."

A few days later he got a call from a friend. "C.W.," the man said, "that transmitter you're planning to buy—it's a piece of junk." The man's nephew, a radio technician, had taken a look at the transmitter and pronounced it worthless. "But he thinks he could build a new one for the same amount of money," he added.

When R.G. LeTourneau heard about it, he offered a corner of one of his factories to build the new transmitter. One day, as the tycoon dropped by to see how the project was going, the radio technician said, "It wouldn't cost much more to double the output on this transmitter to 10,000 watts."

"Do it!" said LeTourneau. "I'll cover the expense."

At the end of their furlough, Clarence and Katherine headed back to Ecuador with a brand-new 10,000-watt transmitter—all because Clarence Jones listened to God's still, small voice and obeyed.

Obedience is learning to listen to God's still, small voice.

FROM GOD'S WORD:

"My sheep listen to my voice; I know them, and they follow me" (John 10:27).

LET'S TALK ABOUT IT:

1. How do you think Clarence Jones felt turning down the chance to build a radio station in the Philippines? Not buying the transmitter?
2. What happened to let Clarence know he had done the right thing?
3. How can you recognize God's still, small voice speaking to you?

LEADERSHIP
The Wake-Up Call

Flicking on his turn signal, Clarence Jones slowed down to turn into the gas station. He and Katherine had just finished a series of meetings in California, and he was looking forward to driving across the United States. A hard-working man, he enjoyed these breaks between overseeing operations at HCJB in Quito, Ecuador, and speaking engagements as president of World Radio Mission Fellowship.

The car in the oncoming lane slowed to turn into the gas station, too. Suddenly, an impatient driver pulled out from behind the other car and stepped on the gas—crashing head on into Clarence and Katherine's car. Clarence hit the windshield and felt his jaw and chest being crushed. The engine was pushed right into Katherine's legs and feet. Blood spurted from a hole in her forehead. "She's dead," he heard an ambulance driver say as his wife was pulled from the wreck.

Katherine didn't die, but she was unconscious for nine days, and doctors feared major brain damage. Clarence couldn't say much because his jaw was wired together in more than forty-two pieces. The doctors said he might never speak again, much less play his trombone. Still, when visitors asked how he was doing, he mumbled, "Romans 8:28." He insisted on sleeping on a cot in his wife's room in case she woke up. When her eyes finally fluttered open, she saw Clarence's swollen, bandaged face. "Why, you're not the Lord!" she exclaimed. She seemed disappointed that she wasn't in heaven.

Clarence mended within a few months, but it took Katherine over a year to fully recover. To everyone's amazement, these two plucky survivors were soon back in the harness again, traveling, speaking, doing radio work, hosting visitors.

The near-fatal car crash made Clarence do a lot of serious thinking. "Katherine," he said, "we both could have died. That would have been all right because we would have gone to be with Jesus. But who would have carried on our work? It's time I began training a younger person to take my place."

Clarence was always encouraging the other missionaries in their work. But now he began looking for specific leadership qualities in his staff:

Aptitude: Knowing what needs to be done.

Attitude: A servant leader who won't ask anyone to do a job you are not willing to do first; a person who depends on God for guidance.

Action: The ability to follow up on what you think should be done and stick with it until it gets done; a person who gets results.

In 1958, five years after the accident, Clarence Jones announced his intention to step aside as president of WRMF, passing his responsibilities on to a younger man, Abe Van Der Puy. The trustees, board, and staff made a special request: "C.W., we'd like you and Katherine to visit all the missionary radio stations around the world while you're still president. Will you do that before you retire?"

Using up "yards of tickets," the Joneses visited seventy radio stations that had followed HCJB's example. They encouraged people already involved in radio and stirred up interest in others. Even as Clarence stepped aside for younger leaders, it was the beginning of a new role as ambassador-at-large for "Mr. Missionary Radio."

A servant leader knows when it's time to
train others to lead.

FROM GOD'S WORD:

Joshua son of Nun was then filled with wisdom, because Moses had put his hands on him (Deuteronomy 34:9).

LET'S TALK ABOUT IT:

1. Why do you think it's important for a leader to train other leaders?
2. What kind of character qualities does it take for a leader to let someone else take his or her place?
3. Do you have leadership abilities? How can you use those abilities right now for God's glory?

GORDON McLEAN

Chaplain to Gang Kids

Gordon McLean's parents had the typical dreams and hopes for their adopted son who was born in Regina, Canada, in 1934. They wanted him to finish school, go to a good college, meet a nice woman, get married, and start a family while he went into politics or business.

But as a teenager, Gordon began attending a Friday evening youth group where he heard the Gospel and gave his life to Jesus. That changed the direction of his life dramatically, and when he finished high school, he told his family that he wanted to go into the ministry. He thought that might mean pastoring a nice little church, but God had other plans. "Finding God's will involves two things," says Gordon, "open doors and wisdom. Look for the first; ask for the second."

For him, the open door involved working for Youth for Christ in Vancouver, British Columbia, where he was asked to visit Frank, a four-teen-year-old boy being held in jail on a murder charge. Gordon didn't want to go, but what could he say? After some small talk, Frank—just a little younger than Gordon—asked, "What did you come to tell me?"

Gordon tried to witness, but Frank knew more Bible verses than he did. In fact, Gordon was surprised that Frank seemed so . . . normal. But when it was time to leave, Frank asked if Gordon could return—and Gordon has been going back to jails ever since.

In time, Frank responded to the Gospel, but he still had to face the consequences of his crime. When he was finally sentenced to life in prison, Gordon was there in the courtroom to support him. It was only the Lord's forgiveness that enabled Frank to be determined to make the best of his situation and witness for Christ in prison.

For Gordon, this was just the beginning. Though a murder conviction might keep a guy in prison for much of his life, lesser offenders usually returned to the streets. Often when Gordon visits one kid, that kid introduces him to someone else, and so the ministry grows. Keeping up with them brought Gordon into their neighborhoods to meet other young people who needed the Gospel.

In 1951, Gordon moved from Canada to the U.S., where the governor of Washington State and a prominent Seattle Christian businessman supported his outreach to offenders. The Lord blessed his ministry, but learning was slow and sometimes painful. Gordon was only seventeen, and it was easy to get too emotionally involved with some of the kids and their concerns.

Wherever God sent him—Washington . . . Montana . . . California—Gordon kept reaching out to kids in jail. Then in 1982, the Lord sent him to work with Metro Chicago Youth for Christ Juvenile Justice Division, where he still ministers to gang kids on some of America's most dangerous streets.

CONFIDENCE
Someone's Looking Out for You

~~~~~~~~~~~~~~~~~~~~~~~~~

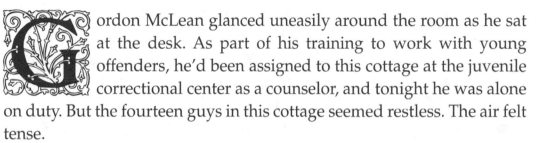ordon McLean glanced uneasily around the room as he sat at the desk. As part of his training to work with young offenders, he'd been assigned to this cottage at the juvenile correctional center as a counselor, and tonight he was alone on duty. But the fourteen guys in this cottage seemed restless. The air felt tense.

Gordon jumped up with a start when a couple of guys got into a fight on the other side of the room. "Hey!" Gordon said, running over to break it up. The next thing he knew, the pair jumped on him and threw him to the floor. Several other young men joined in and held him down. With a sick feeling Gordon realized the fight had been a trick to get him away from the phone so he couldn't call for help.

While Gordon squirmed on the floor, one of the guys went through his pockets until he found the keys to the front door. Another tore a sheet into strips to tie him up.

"Why waste time with that?" yelled one of the boys as he pushed through the group. "Let me take care of him." He raised a crude knife made out of a piece of bed frame. Gordon ducked, sure the guy was going to plunge it into his chest, when someone else stepped forward and caught the guy's arm.

"No!" said the newcomer. "We're not gonna hurt this guy. We want to get out of here, not pick up a murder rap."

But the guy with the knife was determined to stab Gordon. Soon the two of them started fighting each other. Gordon lay helplessly on the floor, looking up as they exchanged blows. If the first guy won, Gordon realized, he'd probably die. If the second guy won, he might get away with his life.

Finally the second kid landed a heavy blow that sent the first one sprawling across the floor. "Now, get up and do what I tell you," said the victor. "We leave him alone, and we get out of here right now!"

All fourteen boys burst out the front door and ran off into the night. Gordon was never so glad to be alone.

Soon another staff member noticed that the door to the cottage was open, and he stepped inside to check it out. Gordon felt a little sheepish as he was cut loose. Once the police were called, it didn't take them long to capture the escapees because they had no escape plan. For one thing, they tried to drive off in Gordon's car—which ran out of gas. When Gordon told the officials what had happened, the two ringleaders were charged with attempted murder.

Later, Gordon visited the guy who had saved him from being stabbed. "Thanks for helping me," Gordon said.

The guy shrugged. "I wasn't doing you any favor," he said. "I just didn't want to pick up a murder charge."

"Yeah, well," said Gordon, "I guess it was Someone else looking out for me. All the same, I'll be in court and tell the judge exactly what went down." Because of Gordon's testimony, the attempted murder charge was dismissed for the young man even though he had to answer for helping to plan the escape.

Gordon cruises streets where at any time he could be caught in the crossfire of a gang war. He has faced down hostile drug dealers and was once caught in a prison riot. He's not so foolish as to enjoy these dangers, but he knows that God is with him and cares for him. "I keep going back," he says, "because that is where the Lord wants me, and I have confidence that He will be with me no matter what happens."

Confidence increases when you know
Someone is looking out for you.

FROM GOD'S WORD:
He has put his angels in charge of you to watch over you wherever you go (Psalm 91:11).

LET'S TALK ABOUT IT:
1. Why did the two boys start fighting over Gordon?
2. If the guy who stopped the other boy from stabbing Gordon was only looking out for himself, who was looking out for Gordon?
3. If you know God is looking out for you, how might that give you confidence in facing a tough situation today?

IMPARTIALITY
"I'm Not Your Judge"

Gordon McLean entered the hospital room with dread. He didn't want to tell Angel that his younger brother, Roberto, was dead. The day before, the two brothers had been the targets of a gang shooting. Angel couldn't talk because his jaw was wired shut so it could heal. But before Gordon could say anything, Angel picked up a note pad and, with tears running down his face, wrote, "My brother. I know."

Angel had started in the gang life at age seven. Soon he knew little else but street wars and drug dealing. He was in and out of the police station and the Juvenile Detention Center until he was finally sent to the Illinois Youth Center at St. Charles on a shooting charge. While Angel was there, Gordon shared the Gospel with him. Angel responded, but conversion seldom produces instant change. A transformed life takes time to develop, and this was no exception.

Before he was really established in God's Word, he was paroled and back out on the streets. Gordon kept up with him, encouraging him along the tough path of major life changes . . . but then Angel and his brother were shot.

In the hospital and later, Gordon got to know Angel's family as they struggled to recover from the tragedy. The police had picked up Pro, the guy Angel said had done the shooting, and the family eagerly awaited the trial, hoping their son's killer would be sentenced to the maximum time behind bars.

Then one day after Gordon had led a Bible study at Cook County Jail, a nice-looking young man came up to him and introduced himself. "On the streets," he said, "they call me Pro."

Gordon gulped. This was the guy charged with killing Roberto and seriously wounding Angel. Pro could tell Gordon was uneasy. "I know how you must feel, you and the victims being friends and all, so I won't bother you anymore." And he walked away.

"W-wait," stammered Gordon before Pro got out the door. Gordon was shaking, but he finally said, "Yeah, they're my friends, but you must not stay away. I'll deal with my feelings, but I'm not your judge. It's my job to share God's Word with you, and I intend to do that."

In the months that followed, Pro became one of the most active, faithful participants in the jail's chapel program. Real repentance seemed to occur.

The night before Pro's sentencing, Gordon went to Angel's house. "There's something I've got to tell you," he said to the whole family.

"Well, go ahead, Rev," Angel encouraged.

"I'm going to be in court tomorrow. I'll be testifying on Pro's behalf. He'll probably get twenty years for murder, maybe more unless I tell the judge how he's been changing through our ministry."

The family sat in stunned silence. Finally Angel's father said, "I thought you were our friend."

"I am," said Gordon. "But I'm also a minister, a pastor, and I have a responsibility to all the young men in my jail group. Only if the judge knows the good as well as the bad can he make a fair decision."

Understanding grew slowly as Angel came over and gave Gordon a hug. Tears welled up in both their eyes when Angel said, "If I was on trial, you'd do the same thing for me, wouldn't you?"

"Yes, I would," Gordon replied.

To be impartial we must often set aside feelings that might cause us to take sides.

FROM GOD'S WORD:

To show partiality is not good (Proverbs 28:21, NIV).

LET'S TALK ABOUT IT:

1. How did Gordon McLean feel when he met Pro? Why?
2. Why did he decide to testify in court on Pro's behalf?
3. It's good to be loyal to your friends, to take their side in disputes, but what should you do if that causes you to be unfair to someone else?

CONTENTMENT
Single for the Lord

hy aren't you married?" kids ask Gordon McLean. Adults wonder the same thing but hesitate to ask, so they don't get the answer. But Gordon doesn't mind telling the kids.

"Why?" he teases. "You want me off the streets? If I was married, I wouldn't have as much time to spend trying to help you stay out of trouble."

Once, Gordon did have plans to get married. He was young and just getting started in his ministry when he met a beautiful young lady and fell in love. His busy schedule of study and travel did not make wanting to get married easy, but they were both determined to make it work . . . at least that's what Gordon thought.

Then one night his fiancée said, "Gordon, we need to have a serious talk. I want a husband who will stay home and be with me, not travel all over the country. You're gone so much of the time! And I don't really want to share my future husband with a bunch of street kids."

Gordon listened carefully as the words sank in. It was one of the saddest moments of his life. He realized he had to make a choice between the young lady he loved and the work he felt the Lord wanted him to do.

That night in prayer he cried, "God, why is this happening to me?" But there was no sudden or dramatic answer . . . just a reminder that God had given Gordon a job.

The engagement was broken. But perhaps as important, Gordon did some careful evaluation over the next few months; he did not want to go through that heartbreak again. Perhaps he would someday meet a woman who would share his vision for the kids. But he also knew that if he followed the path God had set for him, he would be away many nights and odd hours. He couldn't just leave a wife and kids to fend for themselves.

After a man's walk with the Lord, his family must come next. That is divine order and common sense. But there is another route outlined in 1 Corinthians 7, where Paul wrote, "Now for those who are not married . . . It is good for them to stay unmarried as I am" (verse 8). This is not a commandment, but simple wisdom about the challenges of certain types of ministry. For Gordon it was a choice, and he made it. No one urged him to stay single . . . quite the opposite. "You'll get over it when you meet the right woman," people said. But that hasn't happened.

"Aren't you terribly lonely being single?" he is sometimes asked.

"No," he says, so easily that anyone can tell he's really happy. "There is a great difference between being alone and being lonely. I can't recall ever feeling really lonely; a quiet evening away from the pressures and demands of my work is a rare treat I highly treasure. The Lord has more than made up to me in satisfaction whatever I may have lost in not having a wife and family. I have no regrets."

*The secret of contentment is knowing that God will provide
all you need when you are doing what He asks of you.*

FROM GOD'S WORD:

I have learned to be [content] with the things I have and with
everything that happens (Philippians 4:11b).

LET'S TALK ABOUT IT:

1. Why did Gordon's fiancée break up with him?
2. If you were in Gordon's shoes, would you have made the
   same decision he did after this disappointment? Why or why
   not?
3. Describe a situation where you are needing to learn to be
   content.

LOTTIE MOON

From Southern Belle to Chinese Missionary

She was born Charlotte ("Lottie") Digges Moon on December 12, 1840, with all the privileges and prejudices of wealthy Virginian landowners. The Moons were masters of Viewmont, a plantation with fifty-two slaves. Even though her father died when Lottie was only thirteen, education was highly valued in the Moon family, and she graduated with a master of arts from Albermarle Female Institute in 1861. During the Civil War, two of her sisters acted as spies for the Confederacy, and her sister Orianna, the first female medical doctor south of the Mason-Dixon Line, offered her services to the Confederate Army.

Though raised a Southern Baptist, eager, independent Lottie could best be described as "spiritually indifferent" until she was converted during a campus revival at Albermarle in 1858. Following graduation, Lottie wanted to be a teacher, but she longed for a Christian ministry of significance. "Our Lord does not call women to preach," she once wrote, "but He surely commands them as well as men, 'Go work in My vineyard.' " The tiny young woman—she was only four feet three—was fond of Crawford Toy, a Confederate Army officer and later a seminary professor, but she rejected his offer of marriage because of "differences of doctrine."

The "vineyard" for Lottie turned out to be China. In 1873, she sailed on the *Costa Rica* to join her younger sister, Edmonia, in the northern province of Shantung. Eddie's health did not weather the hardships of mission work, and she had to be sent home, but Lottie was to become one of the most outstanding female missionaries of her time.

Getting used to China was not easy for Lottie. At first she considered the Chinese an "inferior race" and Western culture as better in every way. But more important than her prejudices was a sincere desire to lift human beings in spiritual darkness into the light. Leaving the port city of Tengchow, she ventured to the village of P'ingtu, which became her permanent home base. When she put on Chinese clothes to keep warm, she realized people quit calling her a "foreign devil." Before, they were only curious about her American dress; now they listened when she talked about Jesus. Eventually there were enough converts to form a church with a Chinese pastor, Pastor Li.

But the need was so great and the workers so few! Lottie wrote many times to the Southern Baptist mission board and women's groups, urging their financial support to send out more missionaries to China. She fought for "simple justice," insisting that women missionaries should have an equal say in mission decisions and do a wider variety of evangelistic work. During the Boxer Rebellion at the turn of the century, both native and foreign Christians were persecuted, and Lottie had to flee to Japan. When she returned, she risked her own life to encourage the suffering believers in their faith.

Once a privileged "Southern belle," Lottie became "all things to all people so that she might win some." After her death in 1912, the "Lottie Moon Christmas Offering" was collected for missions in Southern Baptist churches and continues to the present day. Her influence on missions earned her the title, "The patron saint of Southern Baptist Missions."

DETERMINATION
The Heavenly Foot Society

ottie Moon couldn't help staring at the tiny, crooked feet of the Chinese women as they tottered down the street with their heavy market baskets. She had just joined her sister Edmonia in Tengchow in northern China, but she was experiencing what the other missionaries called "culture shock."

"Look at their poor twisted feet," Lottie gasped. "How can they even walk?"

"Foot-binding is a product of narrow minds and low morals," sniffed Edmonia, who considered Chinese culture totally inferior to the United States, even in 1873.

"Then the greatest blessing we could give to future wives and mothers is a Christian education," Lottie said boldly.

Lottie Moon had been a teacher back in Virginia, and one of her first missionary tasks was to start a girls' school. It was an uphill battle all the way. The Chinese thought schooling would get in the way of the main business of being female: getting feet properly bound, getting married, and doing all the lowest forms of work. Once Lottie convinced parents to let their daughters come to school, she could hardly bear to see how the girls suffered through the foot-binding process: The four small toes were bent under the foot, pulled toward the heel, and then bound with strips of cloth. Eventually the bones of the foot would break and heal into a small, three-inch foot with a long, pointed big toe. The girls were in constant pain.

Lottie was determined to confront this terrible treatment. To begin, she especially recruited girls with unbound feet as an influence on the other girls and families. As for girls who already had their feet bound, she took every opportunity to free them from this bondage.

One girl's future father-in-law had become a Christian. "Honorable sir," Lottie said to him respectfully, "since this girl will one day be a member of your household, let me unbind her feet as an act of Christian charity."

The future father-in-law agreed. Off came the binding cloths, and Lottie was so happy to see the girl's feet grow normally. But eventually the future groom heard about it and stormed into Lottie Moon's school. "You will bind the feet of my future bride immediately," he demanded. "Do you want to make me the joke of the whole city? A bride with big feet! It is unthinkable."

"I will not," said Lottie. "Your father gave me permission to unbind this girl's feet, and they shall stay unbound."

Furious, the groom stormed out and brought back his father. The father-in-law faltered. "Maybe for peace in the family you should bind the girl's feet again."

The determined spark in Lottie's eye only flamed brighter. "I usually abide by the parents' decision," she said. "But it would be utterly cruel to bind the feet of a girl who is almost a woman. I will not allow such suffering in my school. If you insist, you will have to take the girl out of school."

Again the father hesitated. Seeing her chance, Lottie gave him a personal sermon on how foot-binding was not consistent with his own Christianity. Finally convinced, the father took his grumbling son away, and the girl's feet were spared.

Lottie gave the trembling girl a hug. "One of these days, we will begin a Heavenly Foot Society so that every girl in our mission schools can unbind her feet!" the teacher laughed.

Twenty-five years later, most Chinese Christians and many others supported the anti-foot-binding movement known as the Heavenly Foot Society.

Determination means sticking with what you believe is right, even if it takes a long time.

FROM GOD'S WORD:
Be strong and do not give up, for your work will be rewarded (2 Chronicles 15:7, NIV).

LET'S TALK ABOUT IT:
1. What do you think was the purpose of foot-binding? (Look it up at the library.)
2. Why do you think Lottie Moon thought Christian education was the answer to pagan customs?
3. How would determination help you do something that looks impossible to do or change?

ENDURANCE
On the Road With Jesus

Lottie Moon listened to the moaning wind outside and looked wishfully at her bedroll on the warm kang, a brick sleeping platform. There was a pipe running from the fireplace in the main room to the kang. Shivering, she thought, *Maybe this isn't a good day to begin an evangelistic trip into the country.* She'd much rather stay in her snug little house in Tengchow.

But soon her fellow missionary, Sallie Holmes, was at her door with two sedan chairs, each one carried by two helpers. Mrs. Holmes was a veteran at "country work," but this was Lottie's first trip. The first day they visited six villages, drawing a curious crowd whenever the helpers put down the chairs. "Foreign devils!" some jeered. But others wanted to touch her clothes. Lottie gathered the children into a yard and told them stories about Jesus while Mrs. Holmes taught the adult women. Men hung around the edges of the crowd, listening.

The first night Lottie was so tired, she wanted to fall right asleep. But as she unrolled her bed, villagers crowded into the room, and several women and children crawled right up onto the kang, eager to talk some more. When her voice gave out, the villagers were content to just stand and watch as she tried to eat her supper of mein noodles, onions, and broth.

This happened night after night. After a day of traveling in the sedan chairs and witnessing in six to ten villages, Lottie could barely keep her eyes open. But curious villagers crowded into their room to ask questions: "Are you married? Do you have any children? What—no mother-in-law? Where do you live? How many brothers? Who is your mother? What is that needle for? Who are you writing to?"

One morning as they sat cross-legged on the kang and ate their breakfast of boiled millet and vegetables, Lottie said to her companion, "There are thirty pairs of eyes watching us. I just counted!"

But in spite of the long, weary days, Lottie was amazed at how eagerly the country people listened to the Gospel of Jesus. A roomful of dirty bodies smelled pretty bad, but as she rubbed shoulders day after day with the simple country people, she began to enjoy their sense of humor, friendliness, and eagerness to learn. "I have never gotten so close to the Chinese people since I've been in China," Lottie told Mrs. Holmes one night when the last visitor had finally left them alone. "I feel more and more that this is the work of God."

The two women never knew where they were going to sleep. The inns were filthy, with soot-blackened walls and insects in the mats. One night they slept in a farmer's shed. "Just like Jesus," Lottie frowned, looking around at the cornstalks, tobacco, and farm tools. "No place of His own to lay His head."

Finally the two weary missionaries turned back toward the city of Tengchow. As Lottie was carried in the bouncing sedan chair past the ripening fields, she thought out loud: "Now I understand a little more how Jesus felt walking through the countryside. People crowded around Him every moment, wanting to touch Him, to hear Him speak. He hardly had time to eat! He had compassion for the people and didn't turn them away. But . . . surely He must have gotten tired. How did He keep going?"

Thinking about the Gospel story, she knew: Jesus took time to pray to His Father in heaven.

As the walled city of Tengchow rose on the horizon, Lottie Moon knew where she, too, would get the strength for "country work"—from turning to her Father in heaven.

We develop endurance for our daily Christian life by turning to our only source of strength—the Lord.

FROM GOD'S WORD:

Those who wait on the Lord shall renew their strength; they shall mount up with wings like eagles, they shall run and not be weary, they shall walk and not faint (Isaiah 40:31, NKJV).

LET'S TALK ABOUT IT:

1. Why do you think missionary "country work" was so tiring for Lottie Moon?

2. What do you think "waiting on the Lord" means (see Isaiah 40:31)? How do you think that can "renew our strength"?

3. Name a difficult task that sometimes makes you feel tired and worn out. Try asking the Lord to give you His strength to carry on.

COURAGE
Taking a Beating for Jesus

he young Chinese man got up from his knees in Lottie Moon's little house in P'ingtu City and started to laugh. He laughed and laughed. "I can't help believing!" he cried happily. "I can't help acting out my belief."

Lottie Moon and her new co-worker, Fannie Knight, smiled at each other. God was doing a good work here in P'ingtu and in the surrounding villages. Why, in this year alone, 1889, six converts had been baptized—four men and two women—enough to form a tiny new church in nearby Sha-Ling. And Li, a young Confucian scholar who had become a believer, was now studying the Bible so he could be a pastor.

"God is so good!" cried Miss Knight after the young man had left. "Now we are reaping all the seeds we have sown!"

Miss Moon nodded thoughtfully. "But we must be alert," she said. "Persecution always follows when Satan realizes that the church is growing."

Her words came true sooner than the missionaries expected.

The Chinese New Year—the most important holiday of the year—was in full swing in early 1890 when Lottie Moon heard pounding on the door. When she opened it, there stood one of the new believers from the newly formed Sha-Ling Baptist Church.

"Oh, Miss Moon," cried the woman, "you must come quickly and help us." Her breath came in gasps, and her round face was streaked with tears.

"Come in! Come in!" said the two missionaries. "What has happened?"

With a cup of hot tea to calm her, the woman's story finally came out. During the Chinese New Year celebrations, it was customary to worship one's ancestor tablets. But old Mr. Dan—the first convert in Sha-Ling—would not join in the ancestor worship. All his relatives were so angry, they tied his hands and feet and strung him up on a pole and beat him. "And Mr. Li . . . Mr. Li . . ." The woman began weeping again. "His brothers beat him terribly and dragged him by his pigtail until it tore his scalp from his head."

"Are they—" Lottie Moon cried in alarm, afraid for Mr. Dan's and Mr. Li's lives.

The woman shook her head. "No, they escaped to another village."

"We must send for the United States Consul," exclaimed Fannie Knight. "The treaty that protects American missionaries can protect Chinese Christians, too."

"No," Lottie said firmly. "We must stand for Christ on our own faith, not in the shadow of American protection. Come, let us pray—and then I will go to Sha-Ling."

When Lottie Moon arrived in the village, she went straight to the Sha-Ling Baptist Church, where the frightened believers were gathered. An unruly crowd had gathered outside, making threats. Planting herself firmly between the persecutors and the believers inside, the missionary said, "If you attempt to destroy this church, you will have to kill me first. Jesus gave His life for us Christians. Now I am ready to die for Him."

One of the persecutors drew out his knife and glared at the tiny missionary.

"Come inside, Miss Moon!" her friends inside the church cried. "He will kill you!"

"Only believe, don't fear," she said calmly. "Our Master, Jesus, always watches over us, and no matter what the persecution, Jesus will surely overcome it."

Seeing the small woman standing in front of the church, unafraid, one by one the crowd drifted away, taking the man with the knife with them. But one man turned back and spoke to Lottie Moon. "I saw old Mr. Dan take a beating for what he believed, but he wouldn't change his mind. And I saw you stand up to a man with a knife. Please, I would like to know more about this Jesus who gives such courage."

Acting with courage sometimes helps
others have courage, too.

FROM GOD'S WORD:
Be sure that you live in a way that brings honor to the Good News of Christ. Then . . . I will hear that you are standing strong with one purpose, that you work together as one for the faith of the Good News, and that you are not afraid of those who are against you (Philippians 1:27–28).

LET'S TALK ABOUT IT:
1. Why do you think Lottie Moon did not ask for protection from the United States Consul?
2. Why do you think the man in the crowd of persecutors wanted to learn about Jesus?
3. Do you know someone at school or work who has courage? How does that person influence you?

LUIS PALAU

The Billy Graham of Latin America

Family members were not supposed to phone him at boarding school, so when ten-year-old Luis Palau received a call from his grandmother, he knew something was wrong. "Luis," she said, "your father is very sick. I think you'd better come home." Worried, he was on the train the next morning. But he arrived too late at his hometown of Ingeniero-Maschwitz, Argentina. His father had already died.

Luis Palau had been born November 27, 1934. His prosperous father sold and delivered construction materials. Shortly after Luis's birth, a missionary from the Christian Brethren assemblies led his mother and father to Christ. Their close-knit church provided rich training for Luis and his five sisters. From their earliest years, Mrs. Palau read missionary stories and taught Luis the importance of spreading the Gospel.

To give him a good education, Luis's parents sent him to a British-run boarding school near Buenos Aires when he was eight. The sudden death of his father two years later was a complete shock. "I am so sorry," said his mother, "but it happened so suddenly, we didn't have time to let you know he was ill. He died last night. But I must tell you. At the very last, he sat up in bed and began singing. When he finished, he fell back onto his pillow and said, 'I'm going to be with Jesus.' Then he died."

If Luis were to die then, would he join his father in heaven? The question haunted him until two years later when he gave his heart to Jesus at a Christian summer camp.

Luis's Christian life had its ups and downs, but at the age of seventeen, he faced a choice: go with friends to Carnival Week (where he feared he'd be overwhelmed by temptation) or surrender his whole life to the Lord. With the Lord's help, he chose the latter. Soon he started a job with a bank to help support his mother and sisters. The managers recognized his talent and quickly promoted him.

One day, hearing Billy Graham on radio station HCJB, he prayed, "Lord, someday use me like that to reach others for Christ." From then on he began studying for the ministry. Under the careful guidance of older Christians at his church, he started street preaching.

Later, in 1960 and 1961, with the help of Christian friends in the states, Luis attended the one-year graduate program at Multnomah School of the Bible in Portland, Oregon, where he met and finally married Pat Scofield[6]. After further training (including two months working with the Billy Graham crusade in Fresno, California), Luis and Pat returned to Latin America with Overseas Crusades.

Luis's initial work involved reviving local churches, but in 1965 he conducted his first city-wide evangelistic campaign in a small Colombian town. More than 125 people received Christ. The crusades continued and grew until four years later he conducted fourteen crusades in Mexico, ending in Monterrey, where more than thirty thousand heard the Gospel and two thousand gave their hearts to Christ.

Luis continues to minister throughout the world, having spoken to thirteen million people in sixty-seven nations in addition to hundreds of millions by radio and television.

---

[6]*Two years later Dave Jackson and Neta Thiessen also met each other at Multnomah School of the Bible. They arrived much younger—as freshmen—but their friendship also led to marriage, in 1966.*

RESISTING TEMPTATION
Life Isn't Fair!

~~~~~~~~~~~~~~~~~~~~~~~~~~~~~~~~~~~~

When life isn't fair—and sometimes it's not—it's easy to get angry with God and think He's not doing His job. But God "send[s] rain to those who do right and to those who do wrong" (Matthew 5:45). Everybody enjoys good things and faces troubles. God is more interested in helping us respond well than in always protecting us from trouble.

One day at school, Luis's art teacher made an unkind comment about Luis's painting. Luis said a bad word under his breath, but the teacher overheard him and sent him to Mr. Cohen, the "principal." Mr. Cohen had run the summer camp where Luis had accepted Christ and had been Luis's friend. But when Luis appeared in his office, Mr. Cohen responded very harshly and gave him six hard swats with the paddle. They stung so badly that Luis could hardly sit down and slept on his stomach for a week.

"I only said one little word," grumbled Luis. "Besides, that art teacher started it with his remark about my picture!" When a person is treated unfairly, God cares and wants to help us respond in a good way, but Satan wants us to blame God. Luis let his hurt turn into hatred of Mr. Cohen and anger toward God. *If God doesn't care enough about me to make life fair, why should I care about Him?* Luis thought, and he quit going to

Bible club.

He still considered himself a Christian, but his relationship with Jesus was damaged. His interests switched to other things—car racing, soccer games, school parties—things that weren't necessarily wrong, but they replaced God. He took up with old friends and began talking "rough" and had an uncaring attitude.

Because of his father's death, the family business was failing, and that meant there was no more money for him to finish school. Luis began to blame these hardships on God. As a result, he became depressed and felt sorry for himself.

It was a dangerous time for him spiritually. If his friends had encouraged him to get involved in serious sin, he wouldn't have had the ability to resist. Sometimes young people don't understand why their parents get so concerned about the kind of friends they hang out with. "We're not doing anything wrong. What's the matter, don't you trust me?" they complain. But wise adults know that sometimes we all go through periods when we feel so hurt and forgotten that we don't have much strength for resisting temptation.

Just before Carnival Week in February 1951, Luis finally realized this danger, too. Carnival in Argentina is like Mardi Gras, a time of wild parties and sinful behavior, and he and some new friends had made plans to "cut loose." But deep in his heart, Luis knew this would be like jumping off a cliff. It wasn't so much the sinfulness of the specific activities; it was his attitude. He wouldn't be able to turn around.

Finally he prayed, "Lord, show me a way to get out of this, and I'll return to you with my whole heart."

The next morning Luis woke up to find his mouth strangely swollen as though he had Ping-Pong balls in it. "God has answered my prayer," he said through his puffy lips. He called his friends and said, "I won't be going to Carnival. Something's wrong with my mouth."

They begged and pleaded, but God had given him a way to escape, and Luis stuck with it. It was a major turning point in his life.

Be careful when you've been treated unfairly.
Satan will tempt you to blame God.

FROM GOD'S WORD:

You can trust God, who will not permit you to be tempted more than you can stand. But when you are tempted, he will also give you a way to escape so that you will be able to stand it (1 Corinthians 10:13b).

LET'S TALK ABOUT IT:

1. What were the unfair things for which Luis blamed God?
2. How did this affect his relationship with the Lord? How did it make him feel?
3. Why doesn't God protect us from all the hardships of life? (See James 1:2–4.)

INGENUITY
The Mile-Long Choir

ven if we get killed, we'll hold the parade," the Christian students told Luis Palau. "All we need is your promise that you'll come help us."

What could he say to such a request?

Luis had come to Colombia in 1964 to help local evangelicals plant more churches. Just a few years earlier, evangelicals had gone through severe persecution, so any public ministry was risky. The approach Christian students adopted was to set up on a street corner, play some music, and preach to the small crowd that gathered, then quickly move to another corner. But the strong opposition in the capital city of Bogotá convinced Luis to locate his headquarters in Cali, a city half the size of Bogotá. Nevertheless, Luis promised the young believers that when the time was right, he'd attempt some kind of evangelistic crusade in Bogotá.

Two years later the opportunity came just before Luis was transferred to Mexico. The plan was to have a large parade down the streets of Bogotá to open a four-day crusade. "We can get thousands of Christian young people to come into the city for the parade," said one of the leaders.

"But isn't the government likely to feel threatened by such a crowd?" someone else asked.

"Possibly," admitted Luis. "So we must do everything to make sure we don't look like a mob. We must stay in line no more than four people wide, and we'll sing Christian songs the whole time."

"But how will we keep together?" one of the leaders asked. "Even if we knew what song to sing and when to start, people half a block away would get all out of time with each other. It would just sound like a roar, and no one could hear the words." It seemed like an impossible—and probably dangerous—problem.

Luis and the students thought and thought. Finally they came up with an ingenious solution. "We'll buy airtime on a local radio station and have the station broadcast Christian songs all during the parade. The marchers can carry transistor radios and sing along."

On the day of the parade, ten thousand Christians gathered in the city and lined up in a column four people wide, twelve blocks long. When the songs were broadcast, off they marched, singing in perfect unison as one gigantic, mile-long choir. All along the way the people could hear them clearly, and a huge crowd of observers began to follow.

When the police arrived, instead of trying to stop the parade, they drove ahead and cleared the intersections for the marchers until they arrived at the presidential plaza, where the newspapers estimated thirty thousand gathered. Even the president came out and asked what was going on. "If you can draw crowds like that," he said to Luis, "you could get elected to office." But of course, that was not Luis's goal.

Luis began to preach, and when he finished, three hundred people raised their hands saying that they wanted to be saved. During the next four nights, thousands more heard the Gospel, and there were hundreds of conversions.

This was the rainy season in Bogotá, and it had rained hard every day for a month, but the young people prayed that the outdoor meetings would not be disrupted by rain. And God held back the rain during every service.

*Ingenuity is using our God-given intelligence to
solve an otherwise impossible problem.*

FROM GOD'S WORD:

Good sense will protect you; understanding will guard you
(Proverbs 2:11).

LET'S TALK ABOUT IT:

1. Why do you think the young Christians wanted to hold a
parade to start off the crusade in Bogotá?
2. How do you think the marchers felt when the police came
driving up? How do you think their feelings changed when
the police went to the front of the parade and helped direct
traffic?
3. Name various ways ingenuity has been used in your
church to help spread the Gospel.

SURRENDER
"Say Yes, Chicago"

hen Luis Palau flew into Chicago's O'Hare International Airport in early April 1996 to begin the "Say Yes, Chicago" campaign, no crowds awaited him, and the media paid no attention. But he was expected! Eighteen hundred churches in the greater Chicago area had raised $2.3 million dollars and trained twelve thousand Christians in a two-hour seminar on how to share their faith with others and lead them to Christ. These would be volunteers for one of Luis's most ambitious campaigns to date. The goal was to reach 500,000 people in the fifty-seven-day-long crusade.

But after seventy-five events, some found the results disappointing. Only 129,000—slightly more than one quarter of the original goal—had attended.

Years before—in 1960 at Multnomah School of the Bible—Luis had learned a lesson that applied to these circumstances. God's work was not dependent on Luis's efforts or apparent success. It was not Luis's job to make anything happen on his own.

During a chapel service at Multnomah, Major Ian Thomas, founder of the Torchbearers in England, spoke on the theme, "Any Old Bush Will Do, As Long As God Is in the Bush." Thomas pointed out that it took Moses forty years in the wilderness to realize he was nothing. God was trying to tell Moses, "I don't need a pretty bush or an educated bush or an eloquent bush. If I am going to use you, I am going to use you. It will not be you doing something for Me, but Me doing something through you."

Listening to Ian Thomas, Luis realized that he was like that bush. He could do nothing for God. All his reading, studying, asking questions, and efforts to be successful were worthless. Everything in his ministry would be worthless unless God did the work! Only God could make something happen, and what God intended to accomplish might not even impress people. The secret to being a successful ambassador for Christ was depending on the indwelling, resurrected, almighty Lord Jesus Christ, and not on oneself. Luis needed to be willing to be burned up, burned out, or not burn at all in a way that impressed others.

Thirty-six years later in Chicago, Luis still had to rely on Christ and not on the external measures of success. He knew that he could not experience victory through self-effort any more than he could work for his salvation.

The truth was that even though the overall attendance at "Say Yes, Chicago" was less than expected, God had done what He wanted to do in the lives of individual people. After all, each individual person—one at a time—is who God cares about. One teenage girl had come to the crusade from the suburbs by bus. She didn't go forward after the service because she was afraid the bus would leave without her. But on the way home she talked to a counselor and received Christ. The counselor then talked to the other kids on the bus, and nine more gave their lives to Christ, too. God was not so interested in how many thousands attended as He was in the twelve Chicago street-gang members who came one night and gave their lives to Christ.

Even though the overall attendance was lower than hoped, nearly ten thousand people made public statements of commitment to Jesus Christ—one at a time.

*Surrender means letting God work through
me to do what He chooses rather than me trying
to do what I want for Him.*

FROM GOD'S WORD:

"I [Jesus] am the vine, you are the branches. Those who abide in me and I in them bear much fruit, because apart from me you can do nothing" (John 15:5, NRSV).

LET'S TALK ABOUT IT:

1. How do you think Luis Palau might have felt when several of the large stadium events were only partly full?

2. What had he learned many years before that helped him to not become discouraged by what some might call a disappointing attendance?

3. What do you think Jesus meant when He said, "Apart from me you can do nothing" (John 15:5)?

ST. PATRICK

Missionary to Ireland

Around A.D. 390 (that's about 390 years after Jesus was born), a son was born to a minor British nobleman's family in the town of Bannavem Taburniae. Britain at this time was part of the dying Roman Empire, which had spread Christianity throughout what we know today as England, Wales, and Scotland. The boy was given a Roman name: Magonus Sucatus Patricius. His father, Calpornius, was a local government official and a deacon of the church, and his grandfather, Potitus, was an ordained priest. However, Patrick (as he came to be known) showed little interest in learning God's commandments, much less obeying them. He neglected his studies but loved spending time at the small farm owned by his family along the western seacoast of Britain.

At the turn of the fifth century, Roman troops had been sent to other places, and Britain had been left to defend itself against barbarians from every side. When Patrick was about sixteen years old, a fierce band of raiders from across the Irish Sea attacked the farm and carried off Patrick and many servants and field hands to Ireland. Rudely taken from home and family, he was sold as a slave to an Irish chief named Milchu and put to work tending sheep, cattle, and pigs on a mountainside.

After six lonely years as a slave, Patrick escaped and finally made his way back home. But he was a changed young man. His hardship had taught him to trust in God, and he felt no bitterness toward the Irish people. In fact, he later decided to return to Ireland as a missionary. He began studying for the priesthood, and in A.D. 432 sailed for Ireland to share the Gospel. His work in Ireland earned him the rank of bishop.

Patrick focused his missionary efforts on Ireland's many "lesser kings" (about two hundred of them). He believed that if these tribal chieftains could be won to Christ, the people would follow. When he destroyed pagan idols, he would set up a Christian church on the same spot, replacing the pagan rituals with Christian teaching, worship, and prayers. The druids—advisors to the kings on matters of government and "religion"—were against this Christian bishop, but Patrick's strategy seemed to work. By the time he died around A.D. 461, Christianity had spread and was accepted over much of Ireland.

What is actually known about Patrick's mission in Ireland is largely taken from his *Confessions*, which he wrote in A.D. 450, and a "Letter to the Soldiers of Coroticus." But the *Confessions* are mostly a defense of his mission, not an autobiography or stories of his life. Oral history and storytelling are very old traditions in Irish culture, and many legends and stories have grown up around Patrick's life, which may or may not be based on actual facts. The stories told here in *Hero Tales* were selected as those with basis in actual fact, though the incident of the shamrock is not proved.

After his death, the Catholic Church declared Patrick a "saint," and his influence in Ireland is still felt today.

TRUST

"Your Ship Is Ready"

~~~~~~~~~~~~~~~~~~~~~~~~~~~~~~~

Flames caught the thatched roof and roared like a torch into the night sky. Sixteen-year-old Patrick felt his way through the smoke and stumbled outside. Shouts and screams filled the air. What was happening? Suddenly a heavy hand grabbed his night-shirt and jerked him off his feet. "Let me go!" he screamed. "Let me go!" The boy fought like a wildcat, kicking, scratching, and biting the rough hands that held him. Rawhide strips were wound around his arms and body, and then he was half carried, half dragged toward the hide-covered boats pulled up on the rocky shore.

Patrick woke with a start, shivering on the stony ground. It was the same nightmare again. Six years had passed since Irish raiders had stolen him from his parents' seaside home in Britain, thrown him into the bottom of a crude sailboat, and sailed across the Irish Sea to this wild and pagan island: Ireland. Sold as a slave to a chieftain named Milchu, Patrick spent his days and nights on the rocky slopes of Mount Slemish making sure Milchu's sheep and pigs did not wander away.

"Oh, God in heaven!" Patrick moaned as the first rays of dawn lit the sky. "I did not listen when my father and grandfather tried to teach me Your ways. Now I am paying for my sins. But I put my trust in You, O God, and in your Son, Jesus. I know You are with me every day and every hour of my bitter captivity."

The nightmare gave way to a deep inner peace, and Patrick seemed to hear a Voice saying, "Soon you will go to your own country. See, your ship is ready."

For days, Patrick thought about the Voice that had spoken to him in his sleep. Was God making a way of escape for him? How would he know unless—

He decided to take a chance and run away. With no money or food, Patrick took off on foot through the bogs and forests that stood between him and the Irish Sea. Danger trailed every step. He might be caught by slave catchers or killed by the wild boars that roamed the forests. But after walking two hundred miles, he arrived safely at a seaport half starving with very sore feet.

A large, flat-bottomed, hide-covered sailboat was pulled up on the shore, and a crew of sailors was making ready to sail when the tide came up. "See, your ship is ready," the Voice had said. Was this the ship? The sailors were trying to load a cargo of shaggy Irish wolfhounds to be sold as hunting dogs, but the dogs were frightened, growling and snapping. Patrick, who had a way with dogs, waded among them, calming this one, giving another a pat, and then spoke to the captain. "Can I work for my passage to wherever you are going?" he asked using the Irish dialect he had learned as a slave.

"Get away from here!" snarled the captain.

Without a word, Patrick walked away from the ship and started to pray. He knew God had led him safely this far; he had to trust Him to get him on board that ship. While he was praying, he heard a voice shouting after him: "Come on, hurry up! We'll take you on!" It was a sailor from the sailboat. Had the sailors seen his way with the dogs and convinced the captain that the young man might be useful?

As the tide came in and floated the hide-covered boat out to sea, Patrick turned his back on Ireland and hoped he would never see it again. In spite of his exhaustion and hunger, his heart was full of thankfulness to God. He was going home a changed man. He had trusted in God, and God had rescued him. Now he would give his life to God and serve Him with his whole heart.

Trust is knowing you can turn to God for help when you have nowhere else to turn.

FROM GOD'S WORD:

Tell me in the morning about your love, because I trust you. Show me what I should do, because my prayers go up to you (Psalm 143:8).

LET'S TALK ABOUT IT:

1. Since Patrick hadn't paid any attention to God when he was a nobleman's son, why do you think he trusted God when he was a slave in Ireland?

2. What do you think Patrick had learned about God from his Christian family, even though he didn't seem interested as a boy?

3. Imagine that you were taken away from your home, family, and everything familiar. What do you know about God that would comfort and help you?

BOLDNESS
The Fire on the Hill

~~~~~~~~~~~~~~~~~~~~~~~~~~~~~~~~~

Author's note: The following story is told in all the ancient biographies of St. Patrick. Some of the details may only be legend, but the core of the story is generally considered to have a basis in fact.

he great Council Feast was about to begin. Long, wooden tables were loaded with roasted boar, mutton, and beef. Servants refilled the cups of wine again and again. Minstrels strolled among the guests, entertaining them with songs and stories.

The Irish High King Loaghaire (pronounced "Leary") looked around him with satisfaction. His lesser kings, nobles, druids, and poets had all gathered at Tara, the seat of the High King, for the yearly council and feast. The work of the council—hearing complaints, solving problems, making laws, reviewing payments from farmers renting the king's land—was finished. Now it was time to eat, drink, and be merry—and afterward to light the great bonfire signaling the end of the yearly celebration.

Just then a servant rushed into the banquet hall and tugged at the High King's sleeve. "O High King, a light is blazing yonder on the Hill of Slane."

King Loaghaire's dark eyebrows drew together. "What?" he roared. "But I have given orders that no fires will be lit this night until I light the great Council Fire! Who dares to defy my orders?"

Sure enough, a bright bonfire could be seen on a distant hill. Calling his advisors, the druids, together, the High King asked what should be done.

"O High King," the druids are supposed to have said, "unless you put out that fire tonight, it will never be put out! And the person who kindled it will lure all the people of your kingdom away from our lore and traditions."

It certainly turned out to be true. For the unlawful fire had been lit by Patrick, the Christian bishop who was determined to bring the light of the Gospel to Ireland's pagan darkness. The night of the Council Feast at Tara was also the night Christians celebrated the events leading to the death and resurrection of Jesus, which traditionally included the lighting of a "Paschal [or Passover] Fire." No decree of a pagan king was going to stop Patrick.

Soon Patrick and his companions heard the thunder of horses' hooves and chariot wheels coming from Tara. The little band on the Hill of Slane could easily have been run down and killed. But for some reason, the High King and his warriors stopped far enough back from the light of Patrick's fire—so they wouldn't be overcome by the stranger's "magic"—and demanded to know who had disobeyed the king.

What happened next has been retold so many times it is hard to know fact from fiction. Some say the king's warriors panicked, ran away in confusion, and ended up killing one another . . . others say the king tried to ambush Patrick and his companions, but all the king saw were some deer going through the forest. Whatever happened, Patrick and his companions were not harmed. King Loaghaire grudgingly came to respect Patrick and agreed to listen to the Christian message. It is said that Patrick picked a three-leaf clover (a "shamrock") to help explain the Trinity: Father, Son, and Holy Spirit.

King Loaghaire never did become a Christian, but many of his subjects did. Truly, the fire lit that night on the Hill of Slane in honor of Christ's death and resurrection continued to burn until all of Ireland had heard the Gospel.

We need boldness to share the Gospel when we confront the darkness of unbelief.

FROM GOD'S WORD:

The wicked man flees though no one pursues, but the righteous are as bold as a lion (Proverbs 28:1, NIV).

LET'S TALK ABOUT IT:

1. Why do you think Patrick went ahead and lit a "Paschal Fire" even though the High King had forbidden anyone to light a fire that night?
2. Why do you think Patrick and his companions were unharmed, even though the king and his warriors outnumbered them and had weapons?
3. In what kind of situations do you need boldness to act like a Christian or tell about Jesus? Pray for boldness to live and speak the truth.

RIGHTEOUS ANGER

Blood on the White Robes

~~~~~~~~~~~~~~~~~~~~~~~~~~~~~~~

The messenger fell at Patrick's feet. "O Bishop!" he wailed, "the new converts—many have been slaughtered! And the women and children taken captive!"

"What?" Patrick cried. Why, he had just returned home from Northern Ireland, where many men, women, and children, all wearing white robes, had confessed Christ as Savior. After baptizing them, Patrick had had to leave, but he could still remember the sound of their rejoicing and singing. "What are you saying? Tell me quickly."

The story came tumbling out in gasping breaths. While the newly baptized were still clothed in their white robes—a sign to everyone that they were new Christians—a band of raiders from Wales had attacked them, killed the men and older women, and carried off the younger women and children to sell in foreign lands.

Grief and anger surged through Patrick. "Those are Welsh soldiers— King Coroticus's men," he said bitterly. "The Welsh are supposed to be Christian people. But I do not call them fellow citizens; rather, they are citizens of the demons because of their evil deeds!"

Terribly upset, Patrick immediately wrote a letter to the raiders, asking them to release the new Christians they had captured. The messengers who delivered Patrick's letter said all the soldiers just laughed when they read it.

Now Patrick's blood boiled with anger. He wrote another letter "To the Soldiers of Coroticus" and asked his messengers to read it in King Coroticus's presence.

"I do not know what to lament more," he wrote, "those who have been slain, those whom they have taken captive, or those whom the devil has mightily ensnared." He warned the murdering raiders that they faced eternal punishment in hell as "sons of the Devil."

Patrick couldn't think of things harsh enough to say against so-called Christians who would attack new believers. "You betray the body of Christ . . . ravening wolves that eat the people of the Lord as they eat bread!" He warned other Christians not to even associate with these murderers. "It is not permissible to court the favor of such people, nor to take food or drink with them, nor even to accept their alms, until they make atonement to God."

Having left his own homeland to come to Ireland and win its people for Christ, Patrick took it personally that some of "his own people" (Wales and Britain were closely related) would make such a vicious attack. These new converts were the fruit of his missionary work. "If my own people do not know me . . . Perhaps we are not of the same fold and have not one and the same God as father, as is written: 'He that is not with me, is against me.' "

The only comfort Patrick could find was knowing that the ones who had been killed were now in heaven. "I grieve for you," he wrote, "but I [also] rejoice. . . . I have not labored for nothing. [Since] this horrible, unspeakable crime did happen—thanks be to God, you have left the world and have gone to Paradise as baptized faithful."

Giving instructions that his letter be read "before all the people," Patrick's anger had a redeeming purpose: "May God inspire [the murderers] sometime to recover their sense for God, repenting, however late, [of] their terrible deed . . . and to set free the baptized women whom they took captive, in order that they may deserve to live to God, and be made whole, here and in eternity."

Anger can have a good purpose if our anger is against sin.

FROM GOD'S WORD:
> God is a just judge, and God is angry with the wicked every day (Psalm 7:11, NKJV).

LET'S TALK ABOUT IT:
1. In what way do you think Patrick was hoping that his angry letter would have a good effect?
2. Can you think of a time when Jesus got angry? Why?
3. What kind of evil in our world makes you feel angry? How can your anger be put to good use?

ROCHUNGA PUDAITE

From Tribesman to Translator

During the British rule of India, the state of Manipur was so remote that it did not have a church, hospital, government school, or post office. The Hmar tribespeople in Manipur were not even listed on the national census. A Welsh missionary, Watkin Roberts—"Mr. Young Man," as the Hmar called him—spent five days sharing the Gospel in a Hmar village. The British ordered him to leave, but one of the converts he left behind was a young man named Chawnga, who became a dynamic evangelist and pastor of his people.

Chawnga and his wife, Daii, raised their children to know the Creator God and His Son, Jesus. Chawnga had a special vision for his second son, Rochunga, who was born in 1927. "You must go to school and become educated," he told Ro when he was ten. "Then you can translate God's Word into our own language."

But going to the mission school meant many months and years of being separated from his family. Ro struggled with the frustrating English language. Many times he was tempted to quit school and become a tradesman and get rich. But finally he graduated from high school, then college, then the university, trying to keep his goal of translating the Bible in mind.

An educated Hmar tribesman had political potential as India gained its independence. Many people wanted Rochunga to help form a new political party and be their representative in the new government. He was tempted to go after a political career—but instead he accepted an opportunity to attend a Bible Institute in Scotland. While there he met Billy Graham, who saw the leadership qualities in this determined young Hmar Christian and helped make it possible for him to attend Wheaton College in Wheaton, Illinois.

While still a college student, Rochunga began his translation of the New Testament, which was finally finished in 1958. "Mr. Young Man"— who was no longer young—wanted Rochunga to take over the leadership of the Indo-Burma Pioneer Mission he had started. On one of Ro's trips to India, during which he helped establish nine village schools, he married a Christian Hmar girl named Mawii, who became a delightful companion and partner in missions, as well as the mother of their three children.

By 1970, under Rochunga's direction, the Pioneer Mission—renamed Partnership Mission—trained 350 national missionaries, started sixty-five village schools, and built a hospital. But communist rebels had been at work among the Hmar tribes, and once again the Hmar people begged Rochunga to show political leadership. Rochunga struggled with how best to help his people, and once again God put his feet back on the path of providing God's Word to people who had never heard the Gospel.

Today, Rochunga Pudaite's vision is known as Bibles for the World, with international headquarters located in Wheaton, Illinois.

TRUTH
Finding Truth in a Tree and Under a Bush

~~~~~~~~~~~~~~~~~~~~~~~~~~~~~~~~~~~~~

Ten-year-old Rochunga sat on the bamboo floor of the little church in the village of Senvon. But his mind was not on the sermon his father, Chawnga, was preaching. Soon he would go to the mission school many miles away. His father said it took six days of walking. Worry knotted his thoughts like tangled vines. He would be very lonely so far from his family. And what if a tiger attacked him as he walked the long jungle paths?

His thoughts were interrupted by his father's strong voice. The Hmars had no Bible in their own language, but most could understand the Lushai translation of John's Gospel. "Having loved his own which were in the world, he loved them unto the horizon," read Chawnga from John 13:1.

But the mission school is many miles beyond the horizon! Rochunga thought with dismay. Does that mean God's love cannot follow me that far? After church, he ran to catch up with his father. "Father, you said God's love is unto the horizon, but if God loves me only as far as I can see, how can I trust Him?"

Chawnga was thoughtful. "Come with me," he said.

Father and son walked beyond the village until they came to a tall oak tree. Chawnga began to climb into the spreading branches.

Rochunga followed. "How far can you see?" asked Chawnga.

"I see the mountaintop where the sky kisses the earth," said Rochunga.

"What would you see if you stood on top of that mountain?" asked his father.

"I . . . don't know," the boy admitted.

"If you journeyed to the top of that mountain, you would look far across the valleys on the other side and see another mountain just like it. And if you walked many days and climbed that one, you would see a third mountain . . . on and on. You see, my son," Chawnga explained, "the horizon is never-ending. There is no place in this world where the love of God cannot reach."

Rochunga never forgot the lesson he learned in the tree. Many times when he had doubts and fears during the long school years, he knew God had an answer, if he only looked hard enough to find it. His faith grew stronger . . . but years later when he went to the university in Allahabad in northern India, doubts began to crowd in.

"Christianity is a backward religion," scoffed one of his professors. "In all other religions, man seeks after God. In Christianity, they say God seeks after man. What kind of God needs to seek after mankind? Their God must be no God at all!"

Rochunga knew the Bible said that God was the "seeker." But why? He felt confused. All the philosophers he read agreed with the professor: "It is people who seek God, not the other way around." Troubled, Rochunga could not get rid of his doubts.

One day he lost his favorite pen. It had his initial R carved in it. All week long he looked for his pen, trying to remember where he had last seen it. Then suddenly, there it was—under a bush where he had been playing badminton.

As he picked up the pen, suddenly Rochunga realized the truth. Why did he seek after his pen all week long? Because it was his pen, and it was lost. The pen didn't seek him. And it was the same with God. God created us; we belong to Him. But we were lost. God came seeking us until He found us.

Rochunga smiled. God had once again shown him the truth—under a bush.

God's truth in Scripture is also revealed through nature and everyday experiences.

FROM GOD'S WORD:

"If you continue to obey my teaching . . . you will know the truth, and the truth will make you free" (John 8:31, 32).

LET'S TALK ABOUT IT:

1. Look up John 13:1. What phrase does your Bible use to express how much God loves us? Why do you think the Lushai Bible used "unto the horizon"?

2. How will we recognize God's truth when we see it in nature or in our everyday experiences? (Hint: Read the first phrase of John 8:31.)

3. Describe something you have learned about God in nature.

SACRIFICE
Good Versus the Best

~~~~~~~~~~~~~~~~~~~~~~~~~~~~~~~~~~~~~

R ochunga Pudaite?" said the messenger. "A message from Prime Minister Nehru."

In awe, Rochunga opened the official-looking document. He had just finished his degree at Allahabad University, but he wasn't sure what God wanted him to do next. Now here was the prime minister asking his help in choosing locations for four post offices in the remote jungle area where his fellow Hmar tribespeople lived, and to recommend four people to be postmasters. It was a great honor to be asked, and the post offices would put the Hmars in touch with the modern world.

When Rochunga returned to his tribal village, a delegation of people from the various tribal villages asked to meet with him. "We want to organize a new political party representing the Hmar people," they said. "We need roads, hospitals, and schools. You have met the prime minister. We need you to help us get organized."

Maybe this is how God wants me to help my people, Rochunga thought. He talked it over with his parents. "But, Rochunga," said his father, "what about translating the Bible into the Hmar language? The people need to read God's Word for themselves."

"This is a way to help our people, too," Rochunga argued.

"True," said Chawnga, "but God has higher plans for you. Go ahead to the convention and organize. But I will go to the mountain and pray for you."

The Hmar delegates met in the village of Parbung to organize a political party. When time came to choose a leader, Rochunga was elected unanimously. "Speech! Speech!" the delegates cried.

Rochunga was amazed at what was happening. He had a good chance to begin a political career right now if he gave an acceptance speech. But he put it off. "The speech must wait," he told the delegates. "I will speak to you tomorrow night."

All the next day Rochunga worked on his acceptance speech. Late in the day a runner brought him some mail. Rochunga opened the first letter. It was from Indira Ghandi, congratulating him. The second was also a letter of congratulations from the governor of Assam. The third piece of mail was a cable from overseas. Curious, Rochunga opened it.

INFORM ROCHUNGA PUDAITE MY FRIENDS AND I WILL PAY FOR INTENSIVE BIBLE TRAINING IN GLASGOW OR LONDON STOP CABLE DECISION. It was signed: WATKIN ROBERTS.

"Mr. Young Man!" Rochunga cried. "The man who told my father about Jesus. I didn't even think he knew who I was!"

Now Rochunga had a real dilemma. Should he accept leadership of the new political party as a way to help his people? Or should he get further Bible training so he could translate the Bible into the Hmar language? Postponing his acceptance speech one more day, Rochunga spent all night in prayer. "O Lord, I truly want to do what You want me to do."

Finally Rochunga quit praying and was quiet. Suddenly, the night crickets and tree frogs all seemed to be croaking together, *Glasgow! Glasgow! Glasgow!*

"Yes, Lord," Rochunga prayed. "I will go to Glasgow for Bible training." And immediately a deep peace filled his heart.

The next day when Rochunga told them he would not be their leader, the people were stunned. How could a man sacrifice such a great political opportunity just to study the Bible? But Rochunga knew that political popularity was momentary. God's work is eternal.

Sometimes we have to sacrifice something good
for something better.

FROM GOD'S WORD:
> But [Jesus] did not think that being equal with God was something to be used for his own benefit. But he gave up his place with God and . . . became like a servant (Philippians 2:6–7).

LET'S TALK ABOUT IT:
1. What are some of the good things Rochunga might have done for his people by being a political leader?
2. Why do you think he made the choice that he did?
3. Are you struggling with a choice that seems like a great sacrifice? Pray that God will give you the courage to sacrifice what is good for what is better.

CREATIVITY
"Let Your Fingers Do the Walking"

~~~~~~~~~~~~~~~~~~~~~~~~~~~~~~~~~~

Rochunga Pudaite frowned as he looked at the numbers he'd written on the piece of paper. He had just returned from his beloved India to Wheaton, Illinois, where he headed up the Partnership Mission, which linked American supporters with Indian leadership. In India he had visited many of the schools, hospitals, and churches the mission helped to support. But he came home more aware than ever of the many millions of people who had still never heard the name of Jesus.

"Do you know, Mawii," he said to his wife, "with the average number of people a foreign missionary reaches with the Gospel message, it would take four thousand missionaries a thousand years to tell the millions of people in India about Jesus just once—and that's only if the population didn't keep growing." Ro shook his head. "Sometimes it feels impossible to tell the whole world about Jesus."

Mawii hurried little Mary off to play with her two big brothers and laid her hand on Ro's arm. "You have said yourself that we can't rely on Western missionaries to do the job. We need to reach the educated people in India—the teachers, doctors, lawyers, and government officials—with the Word of God. They are the ones who can then reach the masses of our people."

"Yes. . .but how do we reach them!" Ro said in frustration.

He continued to sit at his desk, alternately praying and brooding. In the background, the radio was playing. A popular advertising jingle for using the telephone yellow pages kept intruding on his thoughts: "Let your fingers do the walking. . . ."

Suddenly, Ro stared at the two telephone directories he had just brought back from India. They listed the names of everyone rich enough to have a telephone in Calcutta and New Delhi. Ninety-eight percent of them could read and write English. These were the very people they had to reach—

"Mawii!" he called out in excitement. "That's it! We'll mail a copy of the Bible to everyone in these telephone directories! And then we'll get the telephone directories for Bombay and Bangalore and—"

Mawii caught his excitement. "If the Bibles come from an Indian citizen, they won't be rejected as just 'white people's propaganda.' "

Starting a fund with $460 of their own savings, Ro and Mawii and their mission staff worked together with Dr. Kenneth Taylor to send copies of his paraphrased New Testament to all the names in the telephone directories. The cover was titled "The Greatest Is Love" and had a picture of the Indian symbol of love, the Taj Mahal. Volunteers typed address labels, included a response card, wrapped packages, and stuck on stamps. Eventually, over 1.2 million New Testaments were mailed to India at a cost of about one dollar per book. More than 200,000 people wrote back saying they were reading the gift Bibles.

"If we can do this for India," said Ro to Mawii and their enthusiastic mission staff, "why not Pakistan. . .Burma. . . ?"

A new mission, Bibles for the World, was born. You can visit its headquarters in Wheaton, Illinois. Maybe you can even help send Bibles to other countries.

*Creativity can use good ideas from the world
around us to glorify God.*

FROM GOD'S WORD:

Every good action and every perfect gift is from God
(James 1:17).

LET'S TALK ABOUT IT:

1. Creative (good) ideas sometimes seem a little crazy. What was "crazy" about Rochunga's idea to reach India's millions?
2. Why was it also a creative idea?
3. Brainstorm some creative ideas to share the Good News with your friends, neighbors, and relatives.

MOTHER
TERESA

Friend of the Poor

She was born Agnes Bojaxhiu ("Boy-ya-jee-oo") on August 26, 1910, to Albanian parents living in Skopje ("Sko-pee-ay"), the capital of Macedonia. Agnes's father, a builder, died when Agnes was only eight years old. But even though her mother, a deeply religious Catholic, had to work hard to support herself and her children, she had a cheerful spirit and taught her children to care about the poor. "If you decide to do something, do it gladly," she said. "Otherwise do not take it on at all."

The Catholic Church was an important part of Agnes's life all through her childhood. She became involved in the Sodality of Mary, a group for young people that learned about missionaries in foreign lands and raised money to help the poor. Their motto was: "What have I done for Christ? What am I doing for Christ? What will I do for Christ?" Agnes decided that she wanted to serve Christ by devoting her life to missions.

At the age of eighteen, she applied to the Order of Loreto Nuns, which sent missionaries to India. In January, 1929, she arrived at the Loreto Convent in Darjeeling, India, as a novice. She chose the name of Sister Teresa, after Saint Thérèse, the patron saint of missions. After taking her final vows of poverty, chastity, and obedience on May 14, 1937, Sister Teresa was sent to the Loreto Convent in Calcutta, where she taught school to wealthy Bengali girls.

But right outside the convent walls was a bustee, or slum. Teresa's heart went out to the hungry children, the sick and elderly dying right in the street, the lepers that no one would touch or help. The sisters tried to bring some of the slum children into the convent to educate them, but convent life was too different from what they were used to. Sister Teresa realized that if she wanted to serve the poor, she would have to go out and live among them instead.

Receiving permission from the pope to leave the convent, Sister Teresa began living among the poor, dressed in a simple cotton sari, teaching the children in the street and comforting the sick and dying. She was joined by some of her former pupils who wanted to serve in the same way. In 1950, the tiny nun formed a new order called the Missionaries of Charity, adding a fourth vow of serving the poorest of the poor.

As head of this order, she became Mother Teresa, and her workers and the work multiplied. In 1960, the work expanded to other parts of India, in 1965 to Venezuela—until today there are more than five hundred centers around the world staffed by the Missionaries of Charity. In 1979, this humble nun received the Nobel Peace Prize and used the prize money to further "the work."

When Mother Teresa died on September 5, 1997, she had become a symbol around the world of "giving a cup of cold water in Jesus' name."

COMPASSION
Jesus in Distressing Disguise

~~~~~~

other Teresa knelt beside the man lying in the gutter of a Calcutta street. His eyelids flickered; his breath came in gasps. He was so thin his ribs looked like a bird cage. The small woman wearing the white sari with blue stripes knew the man was dying.

"Taxi!" she called in Hindi. When a taxi stopped, she said, "Take me to the hospital with this man—quickly." The taxi driver took one look at the man's diseased body and drove off without them. After several more tries, Mother Teresa gave up and borrowed a wheelbarrow from a workman. She lifted the dying man into the wheelbarrow and wheeled him to the nearest hospital.

But the hospital wouldn't take him, either. "We can do nothing for him," they said. "We only have room for people who might get better."

Mother Teresa shook her head sadly and took the man home with her. "No one should die alone and unloved," she told the other Missionaries of Charity. "We need a home where the very ill can die in peace." She went to city officials and asked help in finding someplace to care for the dying. They showed her some rooms that travelers had used who came to visit the Temple of Kali, a Hindu goddess. The rooms were filthy and needed cleaning, but Mother Teresa immediately accepted. She named the new home Nirmal Hriday ("Nir-mul Hree-day"), Place of the Immaculate (Pure) Heart, and went to work cleaning it up. Soon the Home for the Dying was full of men and women no one else wanted to help.

But some of the neighbors were angry. They thought a Catholic mission was corrupting their Hindu temple. One day a group of tough young men blocked Mother Teresa's way. "If you don't leave, we will kill you!" they threatened. Mother Teresa shrugged. "If you kill me, I will just get to heaven sooner," she said. Puzzled that she wasn't afraid, the young toughs backed off.

But still the neighbors complained. These Catholic nuns were going to make Hindus and Muslims into Christians, and that was against the law! They sent a policeman into Nirmal Hriday to kick out the nuns. The policeman strode into the Home for the Dying, ready to do his job. As he looked around the first room, he saw two young women gently washing the dirt from an old man just off the street. Another Sister was feeding a feeble man who could hardly swallow. She had to try many times.

"Don't you get tired?" the policeman asked the young nun.

"How can I get tired?" she smiled. "This is Jesus in a distressing disguise."

Nearby another Sister was tenderly stroking the face of a man with sores all over his body. The man lifted his eyes to the policeman. "I have lived like an animal on the street," he whispered hoarsely, "but I die like an angel, loved and cared for."

The policeman finally found Mother Teresa. She was carefully picking maggots from an open wound in a man's face, talking soothingly to him the whole time.

Turning on his heel, the policeman went back outside. "I will throw out these nuns," he said, glaring at the complaining neighbors, "when your mothers and sisters take their place and do what they're doing for people who are dying."

Compassion is caring for people who are suffering as you would want someone to care for you.

FROM GOD'S WORD:

"Then the King will answer, 'I tell you the truth, anything you did for even the least of my people here, you also did for me'" (Matthew 25:40).

LET'S TALK ABOUT IT:

1. What made it possible for Mother Teresa and her Missionaries of Charity to help people who were dirty, smelly, and diseased without being disgusted?
2. Why do you think the neighbors quit complaining?
3. Do you know someone who is old or dying that you could visit and cheer up?

HUMILITY
Following the
Footsteps of Jesus

The bright blue van made its way through the narrow streets of Calcutta, drove over the Howrah Bridge, which spanned the Hooghly River, and into the area known as Howrah. Finally the "mobile clinic" stopped next to an open lot on the edge of the city where crude shelters had been set up and people squatted near smoky fires or just lay on mats on the ground.

The doors of the van opened, and the driver, Mother Teresa, two of her Sisters of Charity, and an American visitor climbed out, along with a doctor who specialized in the treatment of "Hanson's Disease"—also known as leprosy. As the lepers began lining up for medicine and treatment—all with whitish sores on their bodies, some with deformed toes, fingers, and noses—Mother Teresa said to her visitor, "We estimate that there are thirty thousand lepers in Calcutta. Many of these people could never make their way to a clinic, so we bring the clinic to them."

The American woman tried not to step back from the people clustering around the mobile clinic. In a country where the lowest caste (class) of people was considered "untouchable," lepers were the most "untouchable" of all. In Bible times, lepers had to call out, "Unclean! Unclean!" so that people could avoid coming near them. In India, lepers rang a bell to keep other people away. Anyone who caught the dreaded disease had to leave job and family and live among other lepers. They not only suffered from the disease, but from social embarrassment.

But the Sisters were touching these outcasts and gently bandaging their sores. "Is that really . . . wise?" asked the American woman uneasily.

Mother Teresa smiled. "Jesus touched the lepers," she said. "He humbled himself and made himself like the poor. I would rather these Sisters make a mistake from kindness than work miracles in harshness."

For many years the American woman, a writer, followed the work of Mother Teresa. She was glad when she heard that the "Mother of Calcutta" had established a town for lepers, where they could have decent homes and live with respect. The town was called Shanti Nagar, or "Town of Peace."

Mother Teresa's name and her work gradually became known around the world. Even Pope Paul VI asked her to accompany him on his tour of India in 1965. All those adoring crowds! All those photographers! It would be hard for most people not to let all that fame and attention go to their heads. Why, the pope even gave Mother Teresa the white Cadillac that he had used while in India!

The American woman had to smile when she heard that Mother Teresa had raffled off the Cadillac for 460,000 rupees and given the money to Shanti Nagar. What use did she have for a fancy car?

Many years later, after Mother Teresa—still dressed in her simple cotton sari like a common Indian woman—had received the Nobel Peace Prize, a newspaper reporter asked, "How do you feel about yourself?"

"By blood and origin," she replied with her winning smile, "I am all Albanian. My citizenship is Indian. I am a Catholic nun. As to my calling, I belong to the whole world. As to my heart, I belong entirely to the heart of Jesus."

Humility, as C. S. Lewis said, is not a low opinion of yourself, but a self-forgetfulness.

FROM GOD'S WORD:

It is better to be humble and be with those who suffer than to share stolen property with the proud (Proverbs 16:19).

LET'S TALK ABOUT IT:

1. Mother Teresa was humble because she was always thinking about other people rather than herself. What happens when we "try" to be humble?

2. What is the difference between "humility" and "humiliation"?

3. What would you do if you were given a white Cadillac? (Or won a lot of money?)

BOLDNESS
Even If a Mother Forgets

other Teresa opened the metal gate of Shishu Bhavan, the Home for Abandoned Children in Calcutta. A Hindi policeman stood at the gate, holding a wooden box. "Can you take another one?" he said anxiously.

"Of course," said Mother Teresa, taking the box. She looked inside. A tiny mouth in a small brown face, just barely visible wrapped in the rough cotton towel, made a little squeak.

"Found him in a trash bin," the policeman explained. "Don't know if he'll live."

Mother Teresa nodded. If they could get some nourishing liquid into the baby's stomach, this one might have a chance.

Closing the gate, she moved quickly across the courtyard into the large house. Basketlike cribs occupied the main room. Babies were being fed, bathed, or rocked by Sisters dressed in simple white saris. In the next room, squeals and laughter could be heard as older children played with the toddlers. Some of the children were healthy and strong; others had deformed limbs from malnutrition and disease.

Mother Teresa put powdered milk in a bottle, added boiled water, then sat in a rocking chair, snuggling the thin, little body and humming a song as the baby weakly tried to suck. She thought of all the infants and children that had been left on their doorstep, found on trash heaps, or abandoned when a parent died. The most pitiful of all were the aborted babies, found still alive in a bucket behind a hospital. But every life was precious and worth saving.

Shishu Bhavan was home for about sixty children of all ages. Thousands more still wandered the streets of Calcutta or were abandoned in alleys. But Mother Teresa's Missionaries of Charity gave themselves to each child in their care as if he or she was the only one. They didn't let themselves be paralyzed by thinking about all the children they could not help.

One thing especially upset Mother Teresa: abortion. How could a mother kill her own child? It was unthinkable to her! Regularly she went to all the hospitals and pleaded, "Don't kill the children. Give them to us." Everywhere she preached "Adoption, not abortion." Everyone respected and admired Mother Teresa. But her message about abortion made people who thought women should be able to "choose" whether to have children or not uncomfortable.

Mother Teresa's homes for the dying, for the seriously ill, and for unwanted children spread around the world. In 1979 she was awarded the world's greatest honor, The Nobel Peace Prize, for her humanitarian work. As the tiny nun stood up before thousands of people to give her speech in Oslo, Norway, she didn't care about what was "politically correct" or popular. She boldly said: "Let us thank God on this beautiful occasion, for the joy of spreading peace. . . . But I feel that the greatest destroyer of peace today is abortion. God says very clearly, 'Even if a mother could forget her child, I will not forget you, I have carved you in the palm of my hand' [Isaiah 49:15]. . . . That unborn child has been carved in the hand of God."

Mother Teresa gave a similar message on college campuses, including Harvard University in 1982. She had earned the right to speak "the hard truth" because she lived what she preached. The prizes and honors meant nothing to her. She accepted them because "It is Christ using me as His instrument. . . . To bring all these people together to talk about God is really wonderful. A new hope for the world."

❧

Boldness is having the courage to speak the truth even when it's unpopular.

FROM GOD'S WORD:
We have this hope, so we are very bold (2 Corinthians 3:12).

LET'S TALK ABOUT IT:
1. Why do you think Mother Teresa spoke so boldly against abortion, even though it was very unpopular to do so?
2. What made people listen to and respect Mother Teresa?
3. Consider: Do your love and actions toward others earn you the right to speak boldly?

CHARLES ALBERT TINDLEY

Prince of Preachers

In 1856, on a small farm outside Berlin, Maryland, a little boy was born to a slave couple, Ester and Charles Tindley. The little boy was also named Charles, but his mama died when he was two, and his daddy was unable to care for him. So Charles was "hired out" to other families and farmers to do chores.

Even though the Emancipation Proclamation freed all slaves in 1863, it made little difference to young Charles. His employers were harsh and did not permit him to go to school or church. But Charles had a curious mind. Finding scraps of newspaper along the roadway, he hid them inside his shirt and studied them late at night. Bit by bit he learned his ABC's and taught himself to read. The only book he had was the Bible, and he read it from cover to cover, skipping the words he couldn't figure out.

One day he slipped into a church, trying to hide his tattered clothes and bare feet by sitting in the balcony. But the preacher invited all boys and girls who could read the Bible to come up front to read. Charles sat up. He was a boy who could read the Bible! Ignoring the stares of the congregation, he marched up front and took his turn reading. Everyone was astounded. From that moment on, all Charles wanted to do was learn. He adopted a rule "to learn at least one new thing—a thing I did not know the day before—each day."

During the day, Charles worked as a "hod carrier," toting bricks, mortar, sand, and gravel for construction companies for $1.50 day. After work he went to night school, the "Institute for Colored Youths." He fell in love with Daisy Henry, a local girl, and married her. Hearing about the better opportunities for blacks in Philadelphia, the young couple moved to the big city and found a church home at John Wesley Methodist Episcopal Church (later called Bainbridge Street Methodist Episcopal). Eagerly, Charles agreed to be the church sexton, or janitor. This put him at the church almost daily, where he sat in on Bible classes, talked to the pastor, and read the pastor's books. Making a public confession of faith, he now knew what he wanted to be: a pastor and preacher.

He didn't let the fact that he had little formal education stop him. He studied Greek and Hebrew by mail and finally took the exam to be ordained as a pastor in 1885. After being sent to several other churches in New Jersey, Delaware, and Maryland, he accepted a call back to Bainbridge Street, his "home church," and became its pastor in 1901.

At six feet three, with a strong, low voice and powerful preaching style, Rev. Charles Albert Tindley became a powerful presence in Philadelphia and among Methodist churches. A frequent delegate to the annual and general conferences, he became known as "Mr. Delaware Conference." He built up his church from 130 members to 7,000 members and outgrew several buildings. The worship at his church—and churches everywhere—grew stronger by his over forty-five published gospel hymns. Toward the end of his life, he oversaw the construction of "a beautiful cathedral to give glory to God," which the Methodist conference named Tindley Temple as a way to honor his contributions. When he died in 1933 at the age of seventy-seven, Rev. Tindley had earned the reputation of "Prince of Preachers," by which he is still known today.

HOPE
Heaven's Christmas Tree

While pastoring a church in Wilmington, Delaware, Rev. Charles Tindley visited Philadelphia, his spiritual home. Here he had served as a janitor years before; here he had given his heart fully to the Lord; here he had dug into the Bible, read theology books, and taken correspondence courses (through the mail) in Greek and Hebrew; here he had been ordained as a pastor.

It was Christmas Day, and Rev. Tindley walked the quiet streets, thinking and praying. Passing a large church, he saw the doors open and people coming in and out. Curious, he came closer and through the open doors saw a large Christmas tree trimmed with colorful garlands. All over the tree, colorful packages were tied to the branches.

As he watched, a young man on a stepladder used a rod to lift a package from the tree. As he read the name on it aloud, an excited hand would shoot up from the pews. Rev. Tindley continued to watch until all the packages had been distributed. Boys and girls, men and women, happily passed out of the sanctuary, each with their gift.

And then Rev. Tindley saw a little boy, poorly dressed for how cold it was, one of the last to leave. His pinched face was trying to look brave, but his lip trembled. There had been no package with his name on the tree.

Oh, Father in heaven! Rev. Tindley's heart cried out. *Will there ever be a time when the spirit of Christ shall so fill and control the lives of people that everybody, young and old, rich and poor, will receive some token of love on Christmas Day?*

Almost in reply, a verse in Revelation came into his mind: "Then the angel showed me the river of the water of life. It was shining like crystal and was flowing from the throne of God and of the Lamb down the middle of the street of the city. The tree of life was on each side of the river" (Rev. 22:1–2). Suddenly, Tindley knew God had given him the answer. Jesus is the Tree of Life. He is "Heaven's Christmas Tree" come to earth on Christmas Day with wonderful gifts for every person on earth!

Several years later, Rev. Charles Tindley was back in Philadelphia pastoring the East Calvary Methodist Episcopal Church. At Christmastime he told his congregation the story about the little boy and how God had shown him that Jesus was "Heaven's Christmas Tree." "No one needs to go away empty-handed!" Rev. Tindley preached as he described the following gifts on the Tree of Life:

Hope for the Hopeless. This gift is on the lowest branches of the Tree of Life, within easy reach for everyone. It shines with all of God's promises to sinners and all those who feel discouraged by life's conflicts.

Forgiveness for the Guilty. This gift is the most costly gift, stained with the blood of Calvary. Every single person needs this gift, and there's enough for everyone.

Help for the Weak. Human nature cannot fight against the evils of this world—the temptations of the flesh, pride, and selfishness. But Jesus Christ is stronger than all the temptations of our worldly nature; He is our strength in the fight against evil.

Friendship for the Friendless. A person may be rich in the world's material goods but is poor without a friend. The human soul needs friends, but people often let us down. Jesus is the Friend who will always be there for us.

Peace for the Troubled Soul. God doesn't promise us a trouble-free life. What He does promise is a "peace that passes understanding" in spite of the troubles of life.

Home for the Homeless. Jesus has gone to heaven to prepare an eternal home for every single person who accepts Him as Savior. Regardless of our circumstances on earth, we have a home waiting for us, full of joy and glory.

After hearing Tindley's Christmas sermon, many people in the congregation came forward to receive these gifts from Jesus, the Tree of Life. Year after year, people came from far and wide at Christmastime to hear Rev. Charles Tindley's famous sermon, "Heaven's Christmas Tree." And many people went away with their names newly written in the Book of Life.

The hope we have in Jesus is a gift to be
shared with others.

FROM GOD'S WORD:

Always be ready to answer everyone who asks you to explain about the hope you have (1 Peter 3:15).

LET'S TALK ABOUT IT:

1. Why do you think the little boy didn't have a gift with his name on it?
2. Rev. Tindley used everyday stories to tell about important spiritual truths in his sermons. Can you tell about an everyday event that reminded you about a spiritual truth?
3. Do you know someone who needs to know about the gifts from "Heaven's Christmas Tree"? How could you tell him or her about Jesus, the Tree of Life?

COMPASSION
"No Charge"

~~~~~~~~~~~~~~~~~~~~~~~~~~~~~~~~~~~~~

Rev. Charles Tindley pushed his way past the long line of out-of-work people lined up outside the local "soup kitchen." Times were hard in 1908, and black folks often felt the bite of poverty first as jobs disappeared. The city of Philadelphia responded by setting up bathhouses and soup kitchens in the poorer neighborhoods, but Tindley wanted to see for himself how the need was being met.

The soup was watery; the bread was stale. Rev. Tindley's heart went out to the dejected men, women, and children trying to survive on so little. If this was the best the city could—or would—do, the church ought to step forward.

The next Sunday morning he stood behind the pulpit at East Calvary Methodist Episcopal Church and came straight to the point. "In two weeks the members of this church are going to feed lunch to those without jobs and the hungry at our doorstep," he declared. "Jesus fed the multitudes, and he didn't charge them anything, either. If we are His followers, we must do the same."

The members of East Calvary willingly went to work. The auditorium below the sanctuary was turned into a daily soup kitchen. Local slaughterhouses donated chitterlings, pigs' ears, pigs' feet, gristly beef briskets, and occasional baskets of chickens. When cooked with kale, collard greens, or cabbage, they made a healthy, hot meal. Volunteers cooked, scrubbed floors, washed tablecloths, and helped raise money.

As the weather turned colder, some of the poor who came for lunch stayed till late in the afternoon, when they had to be sent away to make room for evening programs at the church—Bible classes, youth sings, prayer meetings. "It's cold out there, pastor," they said to Rev. Tindley. "We don't have any place to sleep."

Again Rev. Tindley talked to his members. Would they be willing to turn the auditorium into sleeping space for the homeless? It would mean giving up some of their evening programs or finding other places to meet. "Remember what it was like for you and me when we grew up in rural Delaware and Maryland," he reminded them. "We never let a neighbor go hungry or without a place to sleep. Just because we live in the city now, it should be no different. We need to take care of one another."

Many of East Calvary's members shared Rev. Tindley's compassion for the poor. But some of the more wealthy members didn't appreciate the lower-class folks who were beginning to attend church. They wanted to be like the elite congregations over at Cherry Street African Baptist or St. Thomas Episcopal. Rev. Tindley would have none of it. From the pulpit he plainly told these complainers that their attitude was un-Christian. "Jesus didn't seek out the rich and powerful. He ministered to the poor, needy, and rejected." Some of the complainers left the church, but they were quickly replaced by new members from the streets.

But not all the "needy" came to East Calvary's soup kitchen. Two blocks away from the church was a strip of bars, gambling joints, and other "night life." Rev. Tindley often left his study and walked among the drunks, entertainers, gamblers, and prostitutes who strutted the streets. He pleaded with them to leave these sinful pursuits and come to the Cross. Although only a few responded, Rev. Tindley always came back to talk and express his concern. Many on the streets referred to him as "our pastor."

One day a man who was obviously drunk saw Rev. Tindley and greeted him loudly. "Rev. Tin'ley," he slurred. "I wanna shake your hand. You saved me."

Looking the man up and down, Tindley said wryly, "Yes, you look like the result of my work." He knew it was only the saving grace of Jesus who could save such men.

East Calvary's outreach to the poor was reported in one of the city's newspapers. One day the mayor showed up while lunch was being served. Seeing the hundreds being fed, the mayor took Rev. Tindley aside, pulled out his wallet, and gave him five hundred dollars for the work. "This is not a political move," he said. "I don't want one word of this in the newspapers. To profit from the circumstances of these poor folks would destroy any good that might be done. God bless your work."

Compassion is responding to people's needs in the
same way Jesus did.

FROM GOD'S WORD:

When he [Jesus] saw the crowds, he felt sorry for them because they were hurting and helpless, like sheep without a shepherd (Matthew 9:36).

LET'S TALK ABOUT IT:

1. Why did Rev. Tindley think it was Christians' responsibility to feed hungry people?
2. Why did some church members complain?
3. How does your family or church help feed hungry people or provide shelter for the homeless?

PRAISE
The Singing Preacher

~~~~~~~~~~~~~~~~~~~~~~~~~~~~~~~~

Sometimes when Rev. Charles Albert Tindley was preaching about the faithfulness of God to his congregation in Philadelphia's East Calvary Methodist Episcopal Church, he would suddenly start to sing. Then he'd grin sheepishly. "Sorry. Couldn't help myself. Just a little song of mine that's been going around in my head lately."

"Pastor," some of the church members said to him, "you ought to write those songs down. Maybe you could even teach them to the choir to sing."

Music was an important part of worship at East Calvary. The choir and congregation sang a mix of great Methodist hymns and old Negro "slave" spirituals being made popular at that time by the Fisk (University) Jubilee Singers. Some of the older folks, like Rev. Tindley himself, had been born into slavery in the South. But even in the North, blacks struggled with second-class citizenship and prejudice. Many of their ordinary civil rights were still denied. Music was a way to express the deep pain and struggles of life and the saving grace of Jesus that helped them each day.

Tindley's first published hymn in 1901 was an evangelistic song based on the story of Naaman the leper: "Go Wash in the Beautiful

Stream." By 1909, he had published over twenty gospel hymns, such as "Stand By Me" and "Nothing Between My Soul and the Savior."

Three of Tindley's eight children inherited his musical gifts, as well. Emmaline, the middle daughter, broke her father's heart when she had a child out of marriage; but Tindley received his prodigal daughter back home and raised the child as one of the family. Emmaline had a beautiful soprano voice and became a gifted soloist with the East Calvary choir. Her specialty was singing her father's hymns. (She later married a young minister.) Tindley's oldest son, Frederick, a postal worker, could play the alto, bass, and baritone horns, as well as violin and trumpet; he organized an outstanding orchestra at East Calvary. Elbert, the youngest Tindley, was a poor student and a goof-off, but eventually he settled down, using his fine tenor voice as part of the choir and in duets with Emmaline.

Like many other songwriters, Tindley's hymns grew out of personal experiences that flowed out in music. In 1916, he was nominated for bishop in the Methodist General Conference but was not elected. Two more times he was nominated for bishop, but some of his "enemies" were determined that a self-taught former slave without a formal education should not represent black Methodism alongside the white bishops. He was defeated. One of his hymns contains the words, "I often wonder why it is / While some are happy and free / That I am tried and sore oppressed / But it may be the best for me. . . . The Lord knows the way / And I will obey / It may be the best for me." Even in his disappointment, he expressed his faith in the Lord.

One of Rev. Tindley's sons, Sergeant John Tindley, was killed in Europe during World War I. The pastor's grief was poured out in the hymn "I'll Be Satisfied," published in 1919 and dedicated to the memory of his son.

Tindley's associate pastor, Andrew Sellars, organized a men's Bible class at East Calvary. Out of this class, ten men and a pianist specialized in singing Rev. Tindley's gospel hymns in close harmony and became nationally known as the Tindley Gospel Singers. Thomas A. Dorsey, a popular gospel singer and songwriter, credited Charles Tindley with being his inspiration.

But Rev. Tindley did not write music to become famous. He wrote music to express the spiritual truths that helped him endure in his life—a life that began in slavery, was dedicated to sharing the good news of salvation, and was poured out in service and friendship to rich and poor, white and black alike.

Praise to the Lord is often expressed through music.

FROM GOD'S WORD:
Praise the Lord! Sing a new song to the Lord; sing his praise in the meeting of his people (Psalm 149:1).

LET'S TALK ABOUT IT:
1. Do you have any hymns written by Charles Albert Tindley in your church hymnal? Learn to sing one if it's not familiar to you.
2. Not everyone can write music like Rev. Tindley. Name all the different ways people can praise God through music.
3. Read Psalm 150, which could be titled: "Praise the Lord With Music." Choose one of the ways mentioned in this psalm to praise the Lord.

List of Character Qualities ᔑᑫ

AVAILABILITY
   Come When You're Called (Betty Greene)
BOLDNESS
   Even If a Mother Forgets (Mother Teresa)
   The Fire on the Hill (St. Patrick)
CAUTION
   No Old, Bold Pilots (Betty Greene)
COMPASSION
   Jesus in Distressing Disguise (Mother Teresa)
   "No Charge" (Charles Albert Tindley)
CONFIDENCE
   Someone's Looking Out for You (Gordon McLean)
CONTENTMENT
   Single for the Lord (Gordon McLean)
COURAGE
   Taking a Beating for Jesus (Lottie Moon)
CREATIVITY
   Let Your Fingers Do the Walking (Rochunga Pudaite)
DETERMINATION
   The Heavenly Foot Society (Lottie Moon)
DIGNITY
   " 'Whosoever' Means You!" (Mary McLeod Bethune)
DILIGENCE
   No Such Thing as a Menial Task (Mary McLeod Bethune)
ENCOURAGEMENT
   "Make the Seeing Eyes Blind" (Brother Andrew)
ENDURANCE
   On the Road With Jesus (Lottie Moon)

FAITH

    A Slippery Sea of Mud (William Bradford)

    Billy's "Hour of Decision" (Billy Graham)

    "But . . . Where's the School?" (Mary McLeod Bethune)

FORGIVENESS

    The Impossible Letter (Jonathan and Rosalind Goforth)

HOPE

    Heaven's Christmas Tree (Charles Albert Tindley)

HUMILITY

    Following the Footsteps of Jesus (Mother Teresa)

IMPARTIALITY

    "I'm Not Your Judge" (Gordon McLean)

INGENUITY

    The Mile-Long Choir (Luis Palau)

INTEGRITY

    Share One Another's Burdens (William Bradford)

LEADERSHIP

    The Wake-Up Call (Clarence Jones)

OBEDIENCE

    The Piece of Junk (Clarence Jones)

    Revival in a Chocolate Factory (Brother Andrew)

PEACEMAKER

    Saving Squanto's Skin (William Bradford)

PERSEVERANCE

    "Be Like Libby" (George Washington Carver)

PRAISE

    The Singing Preacher (Charles Albert Tindley)

PREPARATION

    Escape of the Duck (Betty Greene)

PURITY

    The Modesto Manifesto (Billy Graham)

RIGHTEOUS ANGER

    Blood on the White Robes (St. Patrick)

DAVE AND NETA JACKSON are a bestselling husband-and-wife writing team who have authored or coauthored many books on marriage and family, the church, and relationships, including the award-winning TRAILBLAZER BOOKS, a unique series of exciting adventure stories that introduce children to inspirational Christian heroes of the past. They have also written the books accompanying the SECRET ADVENTURE video series, the PET PARABLES series, and the CARING PARENT series.

The Jacksons have two married children: Julian, the illustrator for the TRAILBLAZER BOOKS, and Rachel, who has recently blessed Dave and Neta with a granddaughter, Havah Noelle. The Jacksons make their home in Evanston, Illinois, where they are active members of Reba Place Church.